When we hit a wall with one of our kids, we called the Stanleys for advice. Their parenting wisdom gave us clarity, focus, resolve, and the courage to stay the course. After it worked even better than expected, we told the Stanleys they had to write a book on parenting. Regardless of the age of your children, you'll benefit from the Stanleys' insight, experience, and wisdom. Highly recommend!

CRAIG AND AMY GROESCHEL, founders of Life.Church
and authors of *From This Day Forward*

I've often wished for wisdom from those who have effectively raised their kids from toddlers to teens to thriving adult—and for the chance to ask them all the questions. I love that I have found the answers to those questions in *Parenting* by Andy and Sandra. I wish I'd had this book years ago, but I'm so encouraged by it now as I navigate having kids in their twenties. This resource is full of biblically based parenting wisdom from two parents I highly respect. To the moms and dads at any point in the journey, don't miss this resource to help us parents get it right!

LYSA TERKEURST, #1 *New York Times* bestselling author
and president of Proverbs 31 Ministries

I loved this book! In fact, I highlighted notes on every page. At times, I felt like it was so personal that I was reading the Stanleys' journal. The stories are relatable, the principles amazing. No matter the age of your kids, this is the book to read this year.

JIM BURNS, PhD, president of HomeWord; author of *Doing Life with Your Adult Children* and *Finding Joy in the Empty Nest*

Parenting is timeless wisdom from a trusted couple—two parents who have made it to the other side alive (and even happy!). I'm so thankful that Andy and Sandra poured out their cup of experiences, wisdom, failures, and insights so that many generations will be filled up.

COURTNEY DEFEO, author of *In This House, We Will Giggle* and founder of Treasured

PARENTING

PARENTING

GETTING *IT* RIGHT

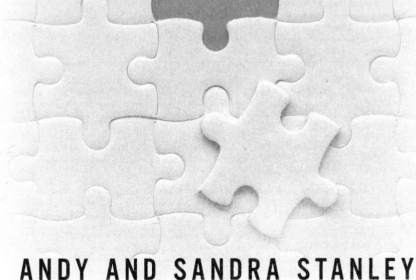

ANDY AND SANDRA STANLEY

**ZONDERVAN
BOOKS**

ZONDERVAN BOOKS

Parenting
Copyright © 2023 by Andy Stanley and Sandra Stanley

Requests for information should be addressed to:
Zondervan, *3900 Sparks Dr. SE, Grand Rapids, Michigan 49546*

Zondervan titles may be purchased in bulk for educational, business, fundraising, or sales promotional use. For information, please email SpecialMarkets@Zondervan.com.

ISBN 978-0-310-36668-3 (international trade paper edition)
ISBN 978-0-310-36629-4 (audio)
ISBN 978-0-310-63866-7 (custom)

Library of Congress Cataloging-in-Publication Data

Names: Stanley, Andy, author. | Stanley, Sandra, 1966– author.
Title: Parenting : getting it right / Andy Stanley, Sandra Stanley.
Description: Grand Rapids : Zondervan, 2023. | Summary: "From North Point Ministries founders and married couple Andy and Sandra Stanley comes Parenting: Getting It Right, a faith-based parenting guide for our times, one that honestly explores the challenges and distinct stages of raising children, while equipping and inspiring parents to lead their families with confidence and grace"—Provided by publisher.
Identifiers: LCCN 2022031564 (print) | LCCN 2022031565 (ebook) | ISBN 9780310366270 (hardcover) | ISBN 9780310366287 (ebook)
Subjects: LCSH: Parenting—Religious aspects—Christianity. | Child rearing—Religious aspects—Christianity. | BISAC: RELIGION / Christian Living / Parenting | RELIGION / Christian Living / Family & Relationships
Classification: LCC BV4529 .S73 2023 (print) | LCC BV4529 (ebook) | DDC 248.8/45—dc23/eng/20220906
LC record available at https://lccn.loc.gov/2022031564
LC ebook record available at https://lccn.loc.gov/2022031565

Cover design: Studio Gearbox
Cover photo: BigNazik / Shutterstock
Interior design: Denise Froehlich

Printed in the United States of America

22 23 24 25 26 27 28 29 30 31 32 33   /LSC/   15 14 13 12 11 10 9 8 7 6 5 4 3 2 1

Contents

Acknowledgments

The names on a book jacket would never get there without a team of people working behind the scenes to ensure there's a book and a jacket to begin with. This book is certainly no exception. An enormous thank-you to Jessica Duquette, Emily Beach, and Holly Duncan. This project was your idea. Thank you for planting the seed, gathering and organizing content, creating our initial table of contents, and writing a few first drafts. To Suzy Gray: your attention to detail and your tenacity in keeping the details in front of us got us to the finish line. To our friends at Zondervan, thank you for believing in this project. We are especially grateful for Kim Tanner. Kim, your edits, questions, and suggestions made this manuscript cleaner, clearer, and crisper. Thank you!

To our amazing parents: words fall short in thanking you for life, for love, for encouragement, and for modeling the kind of parents we strove to be. To Andrew, Garrett, and Allie (along with Ana, Danielle, and Clay): Wow. What an honor to be your parents and parents-in-law. Thanks for your patience with us where we got it wrong and your kindness in letting us know where we got it right. And to our gracious heavenly Father, the only perfect parent: how grateful we are to be your children.

Introduction

It Makes All the Difference

(ANDY)

When Sandra was a senior in high school, she underwent significant back surgery. The results were twofold. She went into surgery at five foot seven and came out at five foot nine, thus ending her dreams of a spot on the American Olympic gymnastics team. The second outcome was that, because of some added hardware, Sandra's surgeon recommended she opt for a C-section if she became pregnant.

From an expectant mom's perspective, a C-section has a couple of advantages, most notably that the mom gets to schedule the delivery, so there is less fear of her water breaking at Walmart in aisle nine while her husband is golfing in a remote location with no cell service. From an expectant father's perspective, the biggest advantage is not having to attend child-birthing classes.

Or so I thought.

We'd been married four years when the parallel pink lines changed our lives forever. By that time, I knew I had married a rule follower. And I'd come to appreciate her by-the-book approach to life. But I was still surprised when Sandra informed me she'd signed us up for four two-hour birthing classes. I say "surprised." "Dismayed" would be more accurate. Why spend four Tuesday nights learning about something I didn't want to know more about and didn't need to know anyway? Technically, she wasn't going to give birth. She was going to have surgery.

No, I did not say that out loud.

Three weeks later Sandra and I were sitting on a blanket on the tile floor of a Sunday school classroom at our church, surrounded by pillows, tennis balls, and a dozen or so other expectant couples. We practiced breathing and pushing exercises. I dutifully memorized my coaching-encouragement script, all the time thinking, "I'm pretty sure the anesthesiologist will ensure none of this is necessary."

When all was said and done, I was glad we attended the birthing classes. As it turned out, the breathing exercises came in handy. For me.

I didn't know it at the time, but just as fathers are encouraged to be in the delivery room for a traditional delivery, they're encouraged to be in the operating room for a C-section. The only time Dr. Lyons looked concerned during Sandra's C-section was when he thought I might pass out.

Homecoming

One additional advantage to a C-section is that mamas generally get to enjoy an additional night of pampering in the hospital. That was nice. But all good things must come to an end. My good thing ended when I heard the nurse say, "Mr. Stanley, if you'll pull your car around to the main entrance, we will bring Mrs. Stanley and baby Andrew down to meet you."

I employed my recently acquired breathing exercises in that moment as well. They were making us leave! But why? Other than the food, everything was perfect here. So why leave now? And why go home? Nobody at our house had any experience taking care of a baby. Surely they wouldn't let us take a baby home all by ourselves.

But they did.

They always do.

As we drove away, the nurse waved goodbye with a knowing look that said, "You have no idea."

And she was correct.

But we figured it out. So did you. By "figured it out" I mean we figured out how to feed, clothe, change, and burp a baby—and eventually get him to sleep through the night. But even with all that ostensible success, there was always this disquieting question: *Are we doing it right?*

If your child is more than five years old, I don't have to tell you that that initial concern never completely goes away. It's why you're reading a book about parenting. You're *pretty* sure you're doing it right. But when it comes to our kids, we don't want to be pretty sure. We want to be sure sure. If there's one area of life we have to get right, it's this one.

So the question is always there, hovering in the background. Then just when we feel like we may be doing it right, the season changes. They outgrow their shoes and their beds and we sometimes wonder if maybe they're outgrowing us. Eventually hormones flip the script. The question that hovered in the background for the first eleven or twelve years is suddenly front and center. We no longer have the luxury of assuming we're doing it right. There are daily reminders that more than likely we're not. And our kids assure us we're doing it wrong because their best friends' parents are clearly doing it right. And, of course, their best friends assure their parents that they're doing it wrong as well.

So are you doing it right?

It's a terrifying question. It's terrifying because while we all come equipped with a rearview mirror, we don't have a reverse. We can look back and see what we should have done differently, but we can't back up and do it differently. Our mistakes are a permanent part of our parenting story. Worse, they're a permanent part of our children's childhood!

Just to encourage you.

Our three children are all married now. Sandra and I still wonder at times if we're doing it right. While writing this book, we've been in a weekly discussion group with five other couples on the topic of parenting adult children. You probably didn't know that was a thing. It is. One day you'll be parenting adults. So, no, parenting doesn't end once they leave the house. Their moving out is just a segue to another season. While the concerns change from season to season, there will always be something to be concerned about. And there is always the concern of doing it wrong.

But what is *it*?

What exactly is the *it* we want to get right as parents? What is the *it* we so desperately don't want to get wrong? Why are you reading a book—or another book—on parenting? Clearly you want to get something right. But what?

Our observation is that most parents are so busy parenting, they never stop to consider what they're parenting *to*. What they're parenting *for*. They're too busy to stop and consider the end game. The goal. The prize. The win. I'm not being critical. We get it. We had three in diapers.

For a minute.

More on that later.

So what is *it*?

What is the win for you as a parent? You have one. Every parent has one. In two-parent homes it's not uncommon for parents to have different wins in mind. When that's the case, they parent at cross-purposes. The result is a tension neither parent can explain but one that children sense and teenagers exploit.

So what's your *it*? What's the win?

Safety? Obedience? Graduation? To make you proud? To get to the NFL? Broadway? To have the things you never had?

To go further educationally than you had an opportunity to go? I coached enough baseball to know that for some the win is for their kids to excel where the parents hoped to but didn't. None of these goals are bad or wrong. But when culled and examined, none of these are enough.

And that's the problem.

So allow me to be direct. Granted, it's a bit early in our relationship for that. But indulge me anyway.

If you don't hit pause long enough to consider the direction in which you are parenting, you may wake up one day to the realization that you parented in the wrong direction. By "wrong" I mean you parented in a direction you would not have chosen had you stopped long enough to choose. This happens all the time. It happens all the time in multiple areas of life. Everybody ends up somewhere in life. The folks who decide on a direction ahead of time usually end up somewhere on purpose. It's the principle of the path:

Direction determines destination.

This is true for parenting as well. We parent in a direction. The direction we choose, consciously or unconsciously, will in some way determine our children's destination. The direction we choose for our parenting has the potential to affect our kids emotionally, relationally, and spiritually, as well as academically and professionally. Sandra and I are foster parents. We've seen this principle play out in the worst imaginable ways. By the time children are removed from their homes and placed in foster care, the parents' influence on the trajectory of their children's lives is heartbreaking and frightening.

You are parenting your children in a direction. You owe it to them to choose it ahead of time.

Not convinced?

Consider this.

If you don't define and choose your *it*, it will be chosen for you. If your parenting style—habits, responses, approach to discipline—is not dictated by a predetermined win, it will be dictated by circumstances, culture, the reactions of your children, and the expectations of others, including your parents and in-laws. Parenting becomes a whirlwind. In the whirlwind, parenting is reduced to *reacting* rather than *leading*, reacting to the immediate instigation rather than leading toward a predetermined destination.

Parenting is complicated. You want to get it right. To do that, you have to determine your *it*. And that's what this book is about.

Sort of.

Actually, Sandra and I would like to suggest an *it*—the *it* we're convinced makes all the difference. It's not original with us. We borrowed it from veteran parents we've observed and done life with over the years, parents who got it right. In that regard, we had two advantages. First, we spent ten years working with middle school and high school students at a local church. For ten years we had a behind-the-curtain look at a variety of family systems and a broad range of parenting styles. I think we saw 'em all: permissive, legalistic, fear-based, helicopter, too involved, not involved enough. We watched parents bail their kids out of situations the kids got themselves into. And we saw parents shrug as if to say, "Sucks to be you."

We took a lot of notes. And we initiated dozens of lunch and dinner conversations with parents who seemed to be doing it right. That process began thirty years ago, before we had kids of our own. Many of the students who were involved in our ministry are still involved with our churches. They're now married with kids of their own. And several students from our youth ministry days are already grandparents. That's three generations we've had the privilege to watch, evaluate, and learn from. And the parents who got it right all had something in common. They shared the same north star. They parented for the same win.

The second advantage we had was Sandra's parents. They certainly got it right. What I saw in them confirmed the core value we observed in the church families we admired most. That core value defined our *it*. We will begin unpacking *it* in chapter 1.

But first this:

Sandra and I don't assume to speak with any authority to single parents or blended families. We both grew up in two-parent homes. But it may help to know that both of our fathers were parented by single moms. Sandra's grandfather died when her father was twelve. My grandfather died before my father turned two. They both lost the influence of their fathers, but both served as excellent role models to their children. They prioritized the same *it*, and it worked.

Again, we know parenting is complicated. You want to get it right. We think we can help. So in the chapters that follow, we'll tell you everything we know about parenting. Not everything there is to know, just what we know. Or to put it another way, we don't assume we can fill your parenting cup. But we're about to empty ours.

Here we go.

CHAPTER 1

Our North Star

(ANDY)

I'm not much of a goal setter. But my dad was. When I was thirteen, he sat me down at his desk with a pen and pad and instructed me to set some goals for my life. Then he left the room. He returned about thirty minutes later to a picture of airplanes bombing tanks, but no goals. We were both frustrated. He was concerned I would meander through life, and I was afraid I would set the wrong goals. Or worse, I would set the right goals and fail to accomplish them. Either way, at thirteen, I thought it seemed prudent not to set any to begin with. So I didn't.

Until Andrew was born.

Here's what happened.

Sandra and I were in the middle of a six-hour drive with infant Andrew strapped into his car seat. We were on our way to meet her parents and siblings for a week at the beach on

Hilton Head Island. For reasons I can't remember, we decided to set some family goals. If a week in one house with members of your extended family is not your dream vacation, I get it. Some families can't spend a weekend together without something going awry.

Not the Walkers.

Early in our relationship I noticed that Sandra's family genuinely liked spending time together. Sandra and her two siblings didn't mind driving two-plus hours to see their parents. And their grandparents. Sandra's brother lived in California for several years. When the family gathered without him, they always called to tease him about what he was missing— usually home cooking and Grandmama's cookies. What was just another day in the neighborhood for the Walkers was new, unusual, and attractive to me.

Their family was drama free and tension free. It was relaxed, enjoyable. On our way to the coast, I brought this up with Sandra. It wasn't the first time. And as was the case every time I talked about her unusual family dynamic, she simply nodded as if to say, "What's your point?"

The point was I wanted *whatever you call that* for our family. Sandra assumed it. But I needed a plan. I'd seen enough to know families don't drift in that direction. They drift the other way. Mine certainly did. My immediate family was full of educated, conservative preachers, teachers, authors, and all-around nice people. But we didn't have what the Walkers had. So I needed a plan. I did not want my family history to repeat itself in our new family. And for things to be different, I would have to do things differently. Think differently. Prioritize differently. It would require intentionality on my part. So we set some goals.

Four to be exact.

Of the four goals we set that afternoon, only one survived the rigors of parenthood. Turns out it was the most important one and the one most closely associated with the dynamic I observed in the Walker family. It has been our north star ever since. It informed every aspect of our parenting—the words we chose, the tone we set, the schedule we adopted, and even our approach to discipline and correction. This was our *it*. And we highly recommend this *it*. We stated it differently back then, and it was longer, but eventually we reduced this big idea to a single, memorable, portable, applicable goal:

> Kids who enjoy being with us and with each other even when they no longer have to be.

Our *it* was relational. Their relationship with us and with each other. Our current and future relationships. So we *parented with the relationship in mind*. If it was good for the relationship, it was good. If not, it was a "thou shalt not."

Raising children who enjoy being with you and with each other even when they're grown and gone may not seem like a groundbreaking concept. It may not be what you value most right now. I understand that. Apart from my experience with Sandra's family, I doubt it would have been my priority either, especially in the early years. When our kids are in car seats or memorizing multiplication tables, who's thinking about when they're grown and gone?

Good question.

Parents who are parenting with "grown and gone" in mind. Parents who are parenting with future relationships in mind. That is precisely why determining your *it* early is so important. Again, if I had not seen *it*, I would not have set my sights on *it* and would have missed parenting toward *it*. I would have missed the opportunity to parent with the relationship in mind in the early developmental years that experts consistently assure us are most determinative. They're the years that matter most and make the most difference. Had I not seen *it*, I'm confident my parenting *it* would have shifted with the seasons. In the end I would have parented toward compliance, competence, and accomplishment. Trust me, I was a fan of all three. I'm still a big fan of competence and accomplishment. But I am grateful that early on we embraced a parenting win that led us to focus on relationship rather than behavior or performance. We're so grateful and we are so convinced this is the way forward that we wrote a book about it.

Beyond our personal parenting experience, we had another compelling reason to write: Dozens of conversations with empty nesters who don't have a healthy, enjoyable adult relationship with their kids, but who want one. Empty nesters who can only imagine what it would be like to gather two or three generations together for a drama-free, tension-free vacation or meal together. By the time you reach our season of life, either you have it or you don't. And if you don't have it, it's difficult to get it. And, I assure you, you'll want it. And your children will need it.

Here's why I say that:

Your relationship with your children, now and later, is determined by the law of the harvest, not the last-minute urgency of the final exam. You can procrastinate and cram for an exam and still do okay. Farmers don't have that luxury. You can't *cram* for a crop. You *plan* for a crop. The farmer who procrastinates . . . well, they don't procrastinate. Heck, they have their own almanac.

There's a season to sow. And there's an optimal time within that season to sow. Good farmers prepare so as not to miss it. As Sandra will explain in the next chapter, there are four primary sowing seasons (stages) for parents. Procrastinate and miss the first one and you'll be playing catch-up.

Again, you can cram for a test. You can't cram for a crop. You sow, water, fertilize, protect, and then wait. And wait. And wait. We remind parents all the time not to grade their parenting until the crop is in. Good news! The crop isn't in at thirteen. Or even eighteen. It comes in around twenty-five. Even perfect parents are no match for a lack of frontal lobe development. So we wait.

Terrifying

The law of the harvest as a metaphor for parenting should strike you as both terrifying and motivating. Terrifying because, unlike with a final exam, there are no second chances. No do-overs. We get one shot per child. Parents joke about making all their mistakes on their first child. Parents with four kids or more joke about the youngest child pretty much raising him- or herself. There's some truth to that. We learn along the way. And if our second born was exactly like our first, all the lessons learned the first time around would be apples-to-apples applicable. But second borns are not copy-and-paste versions of their older siblings. Not to mention, every time we add a child to the mix, the family dynamic shifts. The unnerving point being, we get one shot. We have to get it right—or rightish. That's why *it* matters early.

If you want to get it right the first time, which is your only time, you need to decide what *it* is.

You get what you pay for. And under normal circumstances, you get what you *parent* for. You get what you parent *toward*. You reap what you sow. And once the crop comes in, it is what it is.

No Co-

I would imagine that somebody out there, after reading our *it*, is thinking,

"Sounds like a recipe for codependency."

I get that. It's not. That's covered under "no longer have to be." Besides, as you may have noticed, codependent people don't really *enjoy* each other. They just can't *survive* without each other. Big difference. Independence is an essential ingredient for mutually satisfying relationships. Children who don't fully individuate are robbed of the opportunity to choose an adult relationship with their parents. You can't reconnect with something you never disconnected from. If you parent with the relationship in mind, you will parent your children out of your house and off your payroll. You'll parent them toward healthy independence. They will individuate. They will become their own people.

Like many facets of parenting, moving our kids toward independence is counterintuitive. Parents who let go late or refuse to let go undermine the relationship. This is often the ditch moms fall into. The dad ditch is on the other side of the road. The dad ditch is why many moms are highlighting the portions of this book they hope they can bribe their husbands to read. It's why some of you will read portions of this book out loud to your husbands. That's fine. So, ladies, I'll let you in on a secret that's not really a secret. It's more of an insight. About the last thing we dads want is another dad telling us how to raise our kids, especially our sons.

I know. It's a pride thing, an ego thing. But it's a thing. It's in me as well. The way we think, if it even qualifies as thinking, goes something like this:

> I *have* a dad.
> So I know how to *be* a dad.

Granted, that way of thinking doesn't hold up when it

comes to root canals or prostate exams. It doesn't even hold up when it comes to haircuts. I've had plenty of haircuts, but nobody wants me to cut their hair. Regardless of our flawed logic, it's difficult for most men to admit we don't know all we need to know about raising our children. It's hard to convince us that some fella we've never met and who has never met our kids knows better than we do. So keep highlighting and reading aloud. And remember, moms, your best bet for getting your kids back later is to let 'em go sooner. The goal is not for your children to *need* you. If you need to be needed, you need to see a counselor. The goal is for your children *not* to need you so they can *choose* to be with you. And then when they're with you, you'll know it's because they chose to be.

Dad Ditch

So if moms trend toward hanging on too long, how do dads trend? What's the dad ditch? We dads trend the other way. If we're not intentional, we end up checking out. Sometimes physically. Often *emotionally*, which translates to *relationally*. We become emotionally unavailable. Unreachable. Not on purpose. It's so not on purpose that when someone (usually our spouse) brings it to our attention, we aren't even sure what they're talking about. Dads, if that rings a bell, and you responded negatively, you would do your entire family a favor to initiate that conversation again.

Yes, I'm generalizing. Spoiler alert: There's more of that to come. It's impossible to write on the topic of marriage or parenting without a bit of stereotyping and generalization. I'm a pastor. I am well aware that roles are fluid and the tendencies I'm discussing are sometimes reversed.

So grant me a bit of grace and we will get through this together. I'm confident in your ability to properly contextualize.

Anyway . . . the dad ditch.

Our children are in their late twenties, and two nights ago Sandra initiated one of *those* conversations with me. I always get defensive on the inside. I used to get defensive on the outside.

That's always productive . . .

Almost thirty years into parenting, I have learned a few things. For one, I've learned how unhelpful it is to rehearse all the ways I'm getting it right when Sandra is politely pointing out an occasion when I've gotten it wrong. The other thing I've learned is that taking 100 percent of the responsibility for my emotional or physical absence is always the best way forward. And to say I've had a lot of practice is the understatement of understatements. But in light of our *it*, taking responsibility is the way forward. Being *right* isn't it. Being *understood* isn't it. Healthy relationships with my kids are *it*.

Dads, when we become emotionally unavailable, parenting is reduced to behavior modification. Obedience becomes preeminent. And it works. For a while. It works because we're bigger. That's why it only works for a while. And when it's working, we assume all is well. Our wives know better. But the way we see it, all's well that ends well. They're bathed and in bed, so what's the problem? Why are we even talking about this?

Here's why.

Do you have an enjoyable, nonprofessional relationship with anyone whose focus is how well you behave? No, you don't. Your trainer, golf coach, professional coach—you pay those folks to help you modify certain behaviors. But behavior modification is not the foundation of a healthy relationship. We will talk at length about the importance of obedience, respect, discipline, and everything that goes along with those critical pieces of the parenting puzzle. But for now, remember this: obedience is a means, not an end. Obedience isn't *it*. Compliance isn't *it*. But if you don't engage physically and emotionally, obedience can unintentionally become the *it* toward which you parent. And it will work. But ultimately you will lose. And so will your children. And possibly your grandchildren. Because one or two of your children will likely parent the same way you did.

Having well-behaved children isn't *it*. It's wonderful, especially in public. But that's not *it*. I assume you know better. Most parents know better. But if we're not intentional, if we fail to set our sights on something else, something that positions our children's behavior as a means rather than an end, their behavior becomes an end rather than a means. When that happens, you will find yourself in the unenviable role of referee. Nobody likes the referee.

It's possible to raise well-behaved children who do not enjoy being with you. It's possible to raise well-behaved children who never learn to enjoy the company of their siblings.

It's possible to raise well-behaved children who are unprepared to leave home. It's possible to raise well-behaved children who leave and rarely return—compliant, then absent.

My student ministry days combined with what I experienced with the Walkers led me to conclude that *obedience is a bit overrated*. It's important. But it's not most important. It's essential in the early years. But it's not the north star.

After decades of parenting and now experiencing the payoff firsthand, we're more convinced than ever that the win for parents is healthy adult relationships with their children and healthy adult relationships between siblings—kids who enjoy being with their parents and with each other even when they no longer have to be.

Self-Serving Indeed

I see that hand.

"Andy, isn't this all a bit self-serving? Isn't this about what's best for parents? What about the kids? Shouldn't we parent with their best interests in mind?"

Good question.

It sounds self-serving because it is. But everybody benefits. Everybody wins. Everybody is served. Because:

> Parenting with the relationship in mind leads to better relationships.

So profound.

As we will discover, parenting with the relationship in mind equips our kids to be good at relationships. All relationships.

You've never met a woman whose problems stemmed from a healthy relationship with her father. You've never met anyone who attributed their intimacy issues to a healthy relationship with their parents. I doubt you've encountered an adult plagued by insecurity who maintained a healthy relationship with his father. I could go on and on. Self-confidence, emotional health, and the ability to maintain healthy long-term relationships are just a few of the by-products associated with healthy parent-child relationships. The confidence and emotional well-being associated with intact family relationships equip kids with emotional margin, which in turn sets them up for relational success in every arena of life. That's a win for you as well. In fact, the two most empowering gifts you can give your children are gifts to you as well: a healthy marriage and a healthy relationship. So, yes. Parenting with the relationship in mind is self-serving. But it also equips your children for relational success. A healthy parent-child relationship is the best predictor of a child's relational success outside the family.

You Decide

If you're willing to entertain the notion that raising kids who want to be with you and with each other even when they no longer have to be is a worthy goal, you'll enjoy and benefit from what follows. If not, keep reading anyway because we may convince you. Even if we don't, as you argue with us over the next few hours, you may discover your *it*. That alone would make reading this book worthwhile.

What follows is how Sandra and I got to where we are and what we learned along the way. We'll tell you what we did— the good and the bad. As I mentioned in the introduction, this is not an attempt to fill your parenting cup. It's just our way of emptying ours.

But before I hand you off to Sandra, I want to close this chapter by pointing out an often overlooked but incontrovertible reality that presides like a judge over every aspect of your relationship with your children. It determines what your children *hear* regardless of what you *say*. It regulates how you *feel* regardless of what they *meant*. We include it here because if you choose to parent with the relationship in mind, it's critical that you recognize and embrace this fundamental relational reality.

Your children do not have the same relationship with *you* that you have with *them*.

Keep Your Seat

You are in a relationship with your kids, but it is not the same relationship they are in with you. Not even close. You are relating to a child. Your child is relating to an adult. You are in a relationship with someone who is dependent. Your child is in a relationship with someone who holds all the cards. Those are two very different relationships. It's similar to an employee's relationship with their boss versus a boss's relationship with their employee. It's dissimilar in that adults choose who they work for and who they employ. Neither you nor your child has a choice in the matter. You are the parent. They are your child. Each relationship is permanent. But they're two very different relationships.

When our children are infants, we don't need reminding. They can't do a thing for us, and we do everything for them. But once they begin walking, talking, disobeying, and repeating things they picked up at the neighbor's house, it's easy to lose sight of this parenting maxim. When emotions run high, it's easy to choose words and adopt a tone that don't reflect or support our role in the relationship. The moment a parent gives up their unique role in the relationship, communication becomes unnecessarily challenging and confusing.

With each passing year and each additional inch our kids grow, it becomes increasingly difficult to remember that *the relationship we have with our children is not the same relationship they have with us*—even though they're almost as tall as us, look like us, and, as difficult as it may be to admit, act like us. The practical implications of this relational dynamic are endless. The following four are perhaps the most difficult to keep front and center:

- We shouldn't talk to our kids the way we talk to everybody else.
- We shouldn't *not talk* to our kids the way we *don't talk* to everybody else.

- We shouldn't talk to *all our kids* the same way.
- We shouldn't *argue* with our kids.

We should always choose our words with our role in mind rather than their size, age, or reaction. They may look different than they did ten years ago, but the relationship isn't different, as you're quick to remind them when you feel the reins slipping out of your hands:

"I'm still your mother!"

Translated: Just because you're as tall as me doesn't make you equal to me!

True.

So don't talk to them as you would an equal, a peer, or a friend. Your words weigh too much for that even when your kids weigh more than you. This is why you should never *argue* with your children.

Arguing is for peers.

Arguing is for equals.

You are neither. You are their parent. The moment you step into the ring with one of your children, you have already lost. You've lost because you've allowed your child to bait you away from your unique role. They've maintained their role in the relationship, but you have abdicated yours. It's impossible for you, as a parent, to have an argument with your child. This is why you feel defeated and exhausted when it's over, even if you prevailed. You weren't meant to prevail in your role as a mom or dad. Prevailing is what you do at work, at CrossFit, or at school.

Besides, you can't win an argument with your son or daughter.

"Oh, now I understand! You're right, Dad. I was totally wrong about that. I'm so sorry," said no thirteen-year-old ever.

Including you.

At some point, your kids may attempt to seize control. Sometimes overtly. Sometimes covertly. That's what kids do. It's what you did. When that tension begins to characterize your relationship with one of your children, remember, they don't really want control. They don't really want to be in charge. They're attempting a coup they secretly hope fails in the end. So remain seated. Don't abdicate your unique position.

Your words, whether you're gazing down or up at your son or daughter, still carry enormous weight. Your *no* is a reminder that they're safe because they are not in charge. Your refusal to be their friend will keep the relational lines from blurring, thus protecting their emotional well-being. Your refusal to play the role of friend will pave the way for an adult friendship down the road. Your refusal to change your mind in the face of their tirades will be appreciated, applauded, and perhaps emulated later. But for that to happen, you must remain in your assigned seat—the one labeled *parent*. You are in a relationship with your children, but it is not the same relationship. They will advocate for equity and equality. You must advocate for your unique role in their lives.

Hole in the Wall

Andrew, our oldest, is an introvert by nature. As am I. As is Sandra. The three of us don't raise our voices. When we're mad, we're moody. We don't say anything; we just walk around looking like something is wrong, hoping someone will notice and ask us what's wrong so we can say, "Nothing!"

Garrett, our middle child, is not an introvert.

When Garrett was mad, we knew. Because he respected us, he tried to be respectful. But gearing down when he was wound up did not come naturally. Occasionally, Sandra would send Garrett upstairs to yell into his pillow before they continued a conversation.

Garrett has a thousand friends. He is the most loyal, come-to-your-defense person I have ever met. Garrett has a lot of fun. He has a lot of fun because he is fun. In those ways and more, I wish I were more like him. And I've told him that.

I have two friends, and no one has ever accused me of being fun.

When Garrett entered middle school, I realized that to stay securely strapped in my parent seat, fulfilling my father role, I would need to parent Garrett differently than my dad parented me and much differently than Sandra's dad parented her. I recognized early that Garrett's extroversion, dogged determination, wit, logic, and charm had the potential to draw me out of my corner and thus compromise our relationship.

Growing up, I was not allowed to speak disrespectfully to either of my parents. That wasn't a problem for me. Most of the time I didn't want to speak to them anyway. I just waited patiently in my room until they left the house, and then I would go downstairs and take out my frustration on the piano. Sandra's dad is a Marine lieutenant colonel. You didn't raise your voice in their home either. And you certainly didn't talk back.

As tempting as it was and as comfortable as it would have been to insist on that same posture with all three of our children, I knew if I took that approach with Garrett, we might lose him. Not physically. Relationally. I'd seen that happen too many times during my student ministry days. I was determined not to let that happen with Garrett. And Garrett didn't want that either.

Kids like Garrett relate passionately, persuasively, and sometimes a bit loudly.

No never ended a conversation. It was simply a transition to the next phase of the argument. And while I believed Garrett respected me in his heart, when the pressure was on, he wasn't always respectful with his words.

But I decided that was okay.

I would absorb it. I'm not his friend. I'm not his boss. I'm not his peer. I am his father.

So I chose to let him talk to me any way he needed to and use whatever words he chose to get his point across and his feelings out. He wasn't allowed to talk to Sandra that way. But I was fair game. And that drove Sandra crazy.

"Why do you let him talk to you that way?" she would ask.

Fair question. I let him talk to me that way because I wanted him to talk to me.

The one thing I refused to do—and the reason I'm sharing this story—was argue. I would listen and answer questions. But when I made a decision, I stood by it. And that's usually when things ramped up—when Garrett's diplomacy and charm faded. And he has boatloads of both. But when I gave my final answer, the tone often shifted. I sat there as long as he needed to vent, but I refused to vent back.

Never argue with your children. Arguments are for peers. You're not a peer. You're the parent. Be the parent. If you later discover you were wrong, own it. But don't argue. Parents aren't always right. But parents are always parents.

Late one evening, just before Garrett turned sixteen, he and I had a particularly heated exchange. Neither of us can remember what it was about. I imagine it had something to do with him wanting to go somewhere I didn't want him to go.

"Why, Dad? Just tell me why."

"I've told you why."

"That's a stupid reason."

Probably was.

But it was all I had, and I stuck with it. He didn't like it, but eventually he gave up and stormed off to his room. I was shaken. Sandra walked in with tears in her eyes and said once again, "Why do you let him talk to you that way?"

She knew.

She just didn't like it.

And she knew I didn't deserve it. We chatted for a few minutes before she went back to our room. When she left, I sat there wondering, like I always did, if I was getting *it* right, if this would get us to *it*. Second-guessing is part of good parenting. We second-guess because we care. Because we want to get *it* right. That night, I wasn't so sure. I was all about preserving the relationship. But in the moment, it certainly didn't feel like much preserving was going on. Then I heard someone walking down the hall toward my office. I could tell it was Garrett. So I steeled myself for another round.

Garrett walked in cradling his right hand in his left.

"Dad, I got so mad, I punched a hole in the wall. I think I broke my hand."

I was so relieved.

Not because he busted his hand. I was relieved because he brought his busted hand to me.

Busted hands are what dads are for. That's when I knew we were fine. The relationship was intact. We would survive the turbulence. But to do so would require that I stay strapped in tight to my dad seat. I would continue to be the bad guy from time to time. The "no" guy. And I would be available to help with the busted hands along the way. What he said next was precious and priceless.

"I'm really sorry, Dad. I'll pay to have it fixed."

Garrett didn't hate me. He just hated "no," which isn't a bad thing. Refusing to take no for an answer is how problems are solved and needs are addressed. Turned out his hand wasn't broken. But there was definitely a hole through the drywall. And he missed the stud by less than a quarter of an inch. We measured.

As we stood in his closet staring at the damage, he again brought up paying to have it fixed. I said no.

"Garrett, I don't think we should fix it. I think we should leave it like that."

He didn't ask why. And honestly, I don't know why I chose not to repair the wall. But if you stop by to visit, I'll take you upstairs and show you the hole in Garrett's closet wall.

Remember

You're in a relationship with your kids, but it is not the same relationship. If your north star is a mutually satisfying relationship with your adult children someday, don't abdicate your role along the way. Standing your ground will create tension. Choose to live with it. Learn to manage it. Don't attempt to eliminate it. Just as tension is required to build physical strength, the unavoidable tension between parents and their children builds relational strength. Resolving it now will cost you later.

Be their parent so they remain free to be your child. Don't blur the lines. Stay in your lane. Keep your seat. Your words and your responses will keep everybody in their proper place. You've never heard a story that included, "My parents were amazing. They handed me the reins when I was thirteen. We remain close to this day."

And you never will.

Your children do not have the same relationship with you that you have with them.

Not even close. And that's okay. So remain seated in the parent seat for the remainder of the flight. That will all but ensure your children remain seated and feel secure in their seats as well.

CHAPTER 2

The Four Stages of Parenting

The Early Years

(SANDRA)

It's funny to me that Andy used a farming metaphor in the previous chapter. He'd never seen a farm until he started dating this Middle Georgia girl. We hunt, fish, shoot, and spit.

Okay, I only shoot. I hunted once and didn't get invited back. It was so cold my tears froze on my face, so I started hollering for my dad and scared away all the deer within a three-mile radius.

Fishing is super boring.

And I have a natural aversion to spitting.

But my granddaddy had a farm. That's something, right?

Andy is correct, though. Farmers can't procrastinate. There's no cramming for a crop. They pay attention to the seasons. They study the weather patterns and reports. I can't count the number of times I watched Granddaddy stare up into the sky using all five senses to figure out if rain was on the way. He used every tool and piece of equipment to prep the soil, sow the seeds, and irrigate when necessary. He read and studied and prepared to pivot as changes and unexpected storms came along. He was ready.

Like many soon-to-be parents, Andy and I wanted to be ready too. We read the books and took the classes. There was so much to know. Some of what we learned was helpful. Some of it was not. But one of the first things somebody explained to us was the four stages of parenting. At the time, we thought it seemed like a big deal. Later, we realized it was an even bigger deal than we thought. To say it has shaped most of the moves we've made as parents is not an exaggeration.

The Four Stages of Parenting

The Discipline Years (0–5 years old)
The Training Years (5–12 years old)
The Coaching Years (12–18 years old)
The Friendship Years (18+ years old)

These four stages provide a framework for evolving the parent-child relationship as our kids grow up and move from one stage to another.

In each stage, the approach to parenting is different. We'll tell you what this looked like in our family, but here's the gist of how things should ideally progress.

In the discipline years, you teach your child there are

consequences—good and bad—to their actions. Babies are *not* born knowing this, which is why we put those plastic thingies in electrical outlets, hide toys that are the size of an esophagus, and keep breakable items out of reach. Your role in this season is to strengthen your child's obedience muscle through multiple reps and appropriate consequences.

In the training years, you explain the why behind rules and expectations. You train while you explain. This is the season when you put the wheels on your *it*. You tell your child *what* to do. You explain *why* it's important. Then you help them practice and turn those things into habits.

In the coaching years, you connect more than correct. You loosen the tight reins of the training years and move to the sidelines for coaching. Coaches don't leave the field, and they don't get distracted with other stuff. They watch carefully, call some plays, and pull their players off the field from time to time. They encourage their players to run the plays and respond to situations according to the training that came before. Your goal during this stage is simply to keep them coming to you for guidance and support.

In the friendship years, you hopefully reap the rewards of all that sweat equity. You ramp up to dial back. You're no longer involved in the daily minutiae of your child's life, and your relationship is increasingly free to be a friendship. In this season, you can engage and connect as adults who enjoy each other's company.

All of those stages are fairly intuitive. A basic understanding of child development makes each of them pretty obvious.

But what's not so obvious, and what made this template so instructive to a couple of rookie parents like us, is this:

> Kids move from one stage to the next without thought or effort. But parents don't.

Parents have to consciously adjust their approach as kids seamlessly transition from one stage to the next. Too many parents never do. Or they fall behind and are forced to play catch-up.

You've probably seen a dad who seems stuck in the discipline years. His child may be in middle school, yet he still employs the immediate consequences that were necessary when the child was two, not twelve. Rather than teaching or coaching, he reacts to the first sign of disobedience with instant punishment. He has never moved beyond the first stage of parenting.

Or maybe you know a mom who is stuck in the coaching stage even though her child is grown. She sees their phone calls home as opportunities to offer unsolicited advice and unasked-for opinions. She didn't make the transition to the friendship years.

Even worse, we've all encountered that mom or dad who decides to be friends with their child too early. They neglect training and coaching in an effort to be liked by their kid and their kid's friends. They cave to the urge to prematurely make friendship a priority. And everybody loses.

These kinds of breakdowns ruin relationships. Adult

children who are tired of being told what to do eventually stop calling and coming home. Teens who know they'll be punished stop telling their parents what's going on in their lives. When parents don't evolve their parenting as their child develops, they undermine their influence with their child. Remember, your kids move on to the next stage whether you do or not.

Because of that, the *four stages of parenting* became the road map Andy and I used to build relationships with our kids that we could enjoy once they were grown. That was our *it*. It was a long-term strategy for keeping our parenting on track. And it worked. Did we always get it right? Nope. But this framework informed our decisions and helped us get more right than wrong.

The Discipline Years (0–5 Years Old)

"So, Andy, do you think a two-year-old can be demon possessed?" Seriously, a close friend once asked Andy this.

Here's the story: When Andy and I were blissfully free and childless, we road-tripped to Florida to visit friends. Gathered around the table of a popular seafood restaurant sat Andy and me, our friends, and their two children—ages four and two. The four-year-old boy was quiet and thoughtful, the kind of kid who makes parents think they're rockin' the parenting thing.

But the two-year-old? Not so much. Here we had the kind of kid who leads parents to permanent surgical solutions to ensure there are no *more* kids. Hannah was as cute as they come, but also the strongest-willed kid I had seen to date. She was intent on leading and having everyone else fall into line with her high-chair demands. Also, she was a hush puppy fan.

While we waited for our meals, Hannah blew through her allotted two hush puppies in a matter of seconds. Her dad informed her she was done. "Hannah, you may *not* have another hush puppy." The table grew deathly quiet. Hannah cut her beautiful ice-blue eyes sideways at her dad and reached forward to defiantly palm a third hush puppy, never removing her glare from her father's face.

As the hush puppy traveled toward Hannah's mouth, all other jaws rested on the table in disbelief, including her older brother's. In one swift and smooth action, Hannah's dad whisked her from the table. They disappeared, and the rest of us recovered our composure and returned to nervous conversation.

We didn't know what would happen to little Hannah, but we knew it would be quick and certain. There was no waffling or wondering on the part of her dad about what to do. He had a plan, and this was clearly not their first discipline rodeo.

As we loaded the van to return to their house, the dubious question was whispered to Andy: "Andy, do you think a two-year-old can be demon possessed?" After four years of seminary and graduating with honors upon earning a master of theology degree, Andy answered simply, "Man, I don't know. Maybe."

Funny thing. Hannah is all grown up now and has three little ones of her own, all under five years old. A word about grown-up Hannah: (a) no demon possession, and (b) she's beautiful, smart, successful, and easily laughs about the stories of her childhood. I follow her on Instagram, and I laugh often at the antics of her five-year-old and three-year-old, occasionally wondering if she isn't receiving a bit of payback. Her parents chuckle too.

Fast-forward a year or so from the hush puppy excitement. We headed out to dinner with some local friends. One couple, Tague and Lisa, had a babysitter cancel on them at the last minute, so we told them to bring their three-year-old daughter along. I'm sure it was out of the ordinary, but this little one was having a tough evening. At one point during dinner, Tague decided it was time to address the behavior. He picked up his daughter and left the table to handle the situation. When they returned, their daughter's attitude was noticeably different.

Because we were all close friends, and because two couples—one being us—hoped to soon have kids of their own, we didn't politely pretend nothing had happened. No. We got all up in their business. Where'd you go? What did you do? How did you know what to do and when to do it?

Lisa shared that they could wear themselves out disciplining for every little thing. But that sounded awful. And exhausting. So they decided on three nonnegotiables. This is when they dropped the three Ds on us:

Disobedience.

Dishonesty.

Disrespect.

When their daughter missed the mark on obedience, honesty, or respect, that required attention. The three Ds helped them make quick, in-the-moment decisions about whether to halt everything else and address a situation. Or not. Brilliant!

We didn't forget it, and when the time came for the discipline phase of parenting with our own kids, we adopted this approach. As we navigated the treacherous waters of parenting, we realized that children act childish. That's what they do. Often, childishness requires our correction, but we reserved more serious consequences for the three Ds.

And we intentionally used the words. Even before they could fully understand the meanings, we used the words *disobedient*, *dishonest*, and *disrespectful*. "Allie, when you used your words that way, you were disrespectful to Mommy." "Garrett, when you took that toy and hid it, that was dishonest."

The flip side is that we celebrated like crazy when our kids chose obedience, honesty, and respect. We did our best never to let it go unnoticed. We learned early that *what is rewarded is repeated*. We noticed and celebrated anytime we could. And, again, we used the words.

But back to discipline. These are called the discipline years for a reason. This is the season when our kids should learn—for their safety, for their good, for their future happiness—that there are consequences (good and bad) for their actions. Learning this while the stakes are low? Big win. The older they get, the more severe the world's consequences will be.

Think about this. *Someone* will discipline your kids. It can be you, starting early and being consistent while the stakes are low. Or later it can be a teacher or principal, with consequences like failing grades and suspensions, potentially limiting your child's post–high school options. Or it can be a police officer and judge, with fines, community service, or sadly, jail time or prison. It happens. Even to kids of good-hearted parents. We've seen it. Too often.

Discipline needs to start early. It needs to be consistent. And the consequences during the discipline years need to be immediate.

We disciplined toward, and expected, obedience *the first time*. We didn't threaten or repeat. I know it sounds harsh, but we expected first-time obedience from our little ones. Teaching littles to obey immediately can keep them from physical harm. In some cases, it can save their lives. Sorry for sounding so ominous, but if it takes two or three commands for our kids to obey, it could be too late.

Early on, Andy and I decided never to "count to three" for obedience. We watched parents do that. And if you think about it, it looks silly. "Andrew, come here. I said come here. One. Two. Three . . . Can you hear me? I'm counting . . . One. Two. Oh, good grief. Forget it." Here's what Andrew learns:

1. I'm in control of the big people.
2. If I really don't want to do something, I don't have to.
3. Ignore them and they'll go away.

Again, the stakes get higher as they get older. The teenage

version of it is rough. The adult version can carry lifelong consequences.

While the discipline years can be labor-intensive, they also hold the sweetest memories. Our kids were close in age, and my journals are filled with funny stories, interactions, and hilarious things they said as they interpreted life and the world around them.

Was I tired? Yes. Was I clueless about whether I was doing this parenting thing right? Yes. During these years, at times I felt overwhelmed, isolated, and stuck at home since the effort to load up three kids, four years of age and under, was seldom worth it.

In this season, whether you work full-time or part-time or stay at home, there are some common tensions. There is perpetual laundry and feedings and diapers and more laundry. There's always a part of some child that needs wiping or cleaning. And there's a chronic need to keep everyone busy or contained.

You live and breathe the first steps, first words, and potty training. Maybe you never really worried yourself with safety before, but now it's all you can think about because even if you don't get all the other stuff right, you desperately want to keep them alive another day. You wonder if you're doing enough, and no one can give you the real-time feedback you crave. Also, why in the world didn't anyone tell you how extraordinarily constant this job is? Like, no sick days *ever*.

I vividly remember calling my mom one day to unload some tension. She patiently listened and was appropriately empathic. Then she said something that reframed my thinking: "This is just a season. It will come to a close and turn into memories. I know the days feel long, but the years are short."

She was right. And for the last fifteen years, I've been telling moms everywhere, "The days are long, but the years are short. So don't miss the good stuff!"

With married kids in their late twenties now, I'd love to hop in a time machine and go back for a few days to that seemingly thankless time when kids wanted to snuggle and read and laugh and play but never, under any circumstances, wanted to go to bed.

But I also love this current season with our kids. They all came over for dinner last night. We shared some highs and lows and laughed so hard sitting around the table. We all like each other a lot. They are big and they are fun. And I'm not kidding when I say it's largely because of the hard work of those tedious discipline years. It's worth it. I promise.

The Training Years (5–12 Years Old)

Kerri Strug was part of the "Magnificent Seven" US gymnastics team in the 1996 Olympic Games in Atlanta. Andy and I were there watching her in person, and she was nothing short of amazing. Until that time, the United States had never won a team Olympic gold medal in women's gymnastics.

It was the day for the compulsory round, and the gymnasts were *on*. Each of these outstanding athletes nailed routine after routine. Their bar routines were literally breathtaking. They soared on the floor passes. Even the dreaded balance beam saw nearly flawless compulsories.

And then it was time for the vault.

Cue the music change . . .

Maybe they got too confident. Maybe they got in their own heads. I'll never judge because I was in the stands eating snacks while they did things that seemed humanly impossible.

A teammate over-rotated and landed on her bum. Twice. Turn by turn, each of them struggled for one reason or another.

Now it was Kerri's turn. She gained speed and power as she ran for the springboard. After soaring through the air, she too landed on her rear. But she still had her second vault, and if she nailed it, that would bump out her first score. Walking back to the starting spot, she noticed something wasn't right with her ankle. She had thirty seconds to decide. Go, or no go? Kerri decided to go for it. I mean, you don't get this opportunity every day, right?

She did her same vault a second time. She landed perfectly *but on one foot.* Kerri scored a coveted 9.712, winning the gold for her team and her country. But here's what we found out later. That second vault? She did it with a severely sprained ankle.

I watched an interview with Kerri later. The anchor asked how she was able to pull off a nearly perfect vault with a bad ankle. Her answer was simple. She had trained and trained and trained some more. She had done this vault thousands of times. She had practiced it so many times, her body just knew what to do. And she did it. Now she's a legend.

Talk to any successful athlete about how they do what they do, and they'll tell you the same thing. There's talent, and there's opportunity. But at the end of the day, training is what makes a champion.

So when it comes to parenting, it makes sense that much of the heavy lifting is done in the training years. What do we try to accomplish during this middle chunk of parenting? To be honest, sometimes it seemed enough simply to make it to the end of the week or month or school year with everyone still alive and speaking to each other.

But the truth is, that isn't enough. Expecting our kids to have skills we haven't helped them acquire is exasperating to them. The skills we want our kids to have in public, we must train them for in private. And that's what the training years are for:

> Helping our kids gain the skills and values they need to succeed.

As we said before, these are the years when we explain the why behind the what. There are still consequences connected to actions, but there's a lot more explaining to the training. *Here's what we do. Here's why we do it. Now let's turn those things into habits.*

How?

Practice.

Just as an athlete with their eyes on a gold medal needs tons of practice, so do our kids—we're trying to build them into life champions. We want our kids to be good at the right things. So we practice, and we practice, and we practice some more. Then when life delivers something that takes out an ankle, they'll be well prepared to stick that one-foot landing.

In the Stanley family, we practiced *everything* with our kids. Social skills were a big category. Why? Because social skills are a way to honor other people.

We practiced manners—table manners, conversation manners, all manner of manners. And we used redos all the time. "Oops. Andrew, let's try a redo on that." And we would rewind and try it again. Practicing is great during the early training years because everything is fun and nothing is dumb. Later, everything is dumb and nothing is fun. So do it while you can.

We also practiced greetings. On evenings when we were expecting dinner guests, we would practice answering the door. Andy would go outside and ring the doorbell. The kids would answer the door and practice their "quick draw"—getting their hands out to shake the hands of the guests. We practiced looking people in the eye. We practiced speaking clearly and loudly enough to be heard. Why? Because these are ways to honor people we meet.

This next one is great for the late discipline stage and early training stage. We practiced first-time obedience and made it into a game. Andy called it sending them on "missions." "Here's a mission I need you to accomplish." He'd then give them an instruction or a small chore. They'd respond immediately with, "Yes, sir, Dad!" They were practicing obedience.

Why did we want that? Two reasons. Practicing obedience while kids are young increases the safety factor and sets them up to respond appropriately to authority later.

We had the boys practice holding doors, standing at the table until all the women were seated, and offering their seats if there were not enough chairs for the ladies in the room. Why? Not because we're old-fashioned or think women are weak but because we wanted to train our boys early on to respect and honor women. We also wanted to set the bar high for how Allie would allow men to treat her.

This next one sounds a little weird—we thought so when we first heard about it in a parenting class—but we tried it and realized it was great. It's called the "interrupt rule." Isn't it annoying when you're in a conversation with another adult, and your child or theirs walks up and rudely interrupts the conversation?

The interrupt rule provides a mannerly solution. Rather than launching into whatever your child wants to say, they gently place their hand on your arm and hold it there until you're able to give them your attention. For a small child, they can place their hand on your leg if they can't reach your arm. As soon as you are able, you ask the other adult to excuse you a moment. Then you turn to your child and respond to their request. Teaching this skill can save us from being irritated with our kids over something we didn't train them to do differently.

Why this rule? Not interrupting shows respect and honors others.

At some point while our kids were young, we read about a study called the Stanford marshmallow experiment, a 1960s and '70s study on delayed gratification. The researchers took kids around five or six years old, one at a time, and placed them in a room at a table. Right about eye level for these kids was a jumbo marshmallow. They told the children that they could eat the marshmallow right away or wait fifteen minutes until the researcher came back. If they waited, they got two marshmallows instead of one.

Through the years, they conducted studies to follow up and track this same group. The findings showed that the kids who exercised self-control and waited for the second marshmallow ended up doing better in school, stayed more physically fit, and were generally considered more successful in life by their parents and peers.

While the results were later disputed based on numerous variables not considered, Andy and I still thought it would be a fun experiment to try. So we did. And it was hilarious.

The kids waited, but we could tell it was *really* hard. We didn't assume the kids' response was a predictor that they would always have stellar self-control—we would have been wrong. But it was a fun game, and it gave us a great segue to talk about the importance of self-control and delayed gratification in real life, another skill worth practicing with kids we hoped would be relationally healthy adults someday.

Those are a few of the skills we practiced with our kids during the training years. There were many more, but that should get you thinking. The beauty of this season? Kids love practicing and playing games. They'll play just about anything if it means they get to play with *you*.

So what is most important to you? And what skills and values will get your kids there? Train toward *it*. Refrain from expecting publicly what you have not trained toward privately. And don't miss the opportunities to make the moments teachable. Practice, practice, practice. You're raising some amazing potential champions, and their futures are worth the extra effort.

CHAPTER 3

The Four Stages of Parenting

The Later Years

(SANDRA)

M om! Have you seen my machete?"

This is what Garrett yelled over the balcony ten minutes before our first-ever home inspection for being a foster family. What? Are you kidding me? Wherever that machete was, I was sure the inspector would trip over it, sustain a life-threatening and probably very messy wound, and maybe die in our house. And we'd fail the home visit.

The machete was a recent acquisition from a mission trip Garrett was finally old enough to go on without us. It came from somewhere in the bush in Africa, I think. The moral of the story? Don't let your kids grow up. It's hard. And messy. And often you end up with an arsenal of tetanus-coated weaponry.

The Coaching Years (12–18 Years Old)

But if they must grow up, we have a few thoughts about entering this trepidatious coaching stage where our kids hit puberty and start thinking we know nothing at all. In a flash they move from being our most adoring fans to slinking in the corners of public places so they don't die of embarrassment over us.

Transitions are hard. And to get where we were all trying to go was sometimes a rocky journey. It's a weird time when there seem to be cravings for privacy and independence, a cocktail of hormones, and a newfound insecurity. These all swirl together and deliver a bite when you least expect it.

It's a time when you think the life-changing insight you can't wait to share will be received with wide-eyed wonder. Because, gosh, who doesn't want to be helped? Your fifteen-year-old, that's who. Alas, the days of your kiddos fawning for your attention and help are over. (Temporarily, though, because when the hormone fog lifts, they often revert to valuing your wisdom.)

I'll never forget nearing the end of the training years with the boys. It was like I knew our relationship had to shift to something completely different. I wasn't wrong. And it wasn't easy. They were boys turning into men. I've never been either. I had to adjust my mom approach and let Andy take over the *becoming men* part.

This season looked different for each of our kids. Andrew, our firstborn, with many of the firstborn tendencies, went to his room for about four years. He was *so* quiet, and I didn't like it. Andy assured me it was normal and that I didn't need to take it personally. Meanwhile, he had private conversations with Andrew to remind him to at least glance my way and make a sound as he went up the stairs after school. I was thankful for the morsel.

Garrett experienced this season in rage. Not constant rage. But he was pretty easily ticked off and was unable to camouflage it. Occasionally, I would simply put my hands on his shoulders and ask him to go upstairs and scream into his pillow.

Allie's transition was entirely different. For her, this stage manifested itself mostly in tears. Sometimes when she would cry, I would cozy up to her and ask why she was crying. She would do the sweet "cry-talk" and tell me she had no idea. Do you know about cry-talk? Where every vowel is drawn out three times normal length and the pitch goes up an octave or two?

Allie was self-aware about these changes, and sometimes we would end up laughing. Sometimes not. I had told her a few years earlier that there would come a time when she would cry for no reason and confuse herself and everyone around her. So when it happened, she knew what it was. "I think this is that thing you told me about, Mom," she said in cry-talk.

Transitioning from our parenting approach in the training years to one that looks a bit different in the coaching years might be the most important relational adjustment of all. And trust me, it's not an easy change to make. But allowing your kids increased responsibility for decision-making lays the groundwork for the season to come—you know, the one when you won't be there.

The coaching years are the ones when you stand on the sidelines while they make independent decisions. They're in the game, and you cheer them on. You give some instructions and suggestions, but you hang back, letting them gain personal momentum.

Yeah, occasionally you yank 'em off the field for a few minutes to let them collect themselves or get some rest. But largely, you let them process information and decide for themselves. If you try to force teachable moments or bring back "training" tactics too often, you lose them. They stop talking. They can't wait to leave home because they'll finally have some leeway to succeed, or fail, apart from you.

This is also the season when you do more *connecting* than *correcting*. This was a harder transition for me than it was for Andy. Correcting is my jam. Maybe because I like telling people what to do and harbor secret thoughts that if folks would just do what I say, life would be better for everyone. There's a word for this: pride. But I've learned the hard way that I am, in fact, *not* always right. That still stings a little.

So what does connecting look like? I mean, I think we're clear on what *correcting* is. We've been doing that for a while. Here are three phrases that wrap some understanding around connecting over correcting:

Cultivate constant conversations.

Don't bail; let 'em fail.

Get interested in what interests them.

One thing Andy and I discovered in the coaching years was the importance of constant conversations. This isn't the same as talking your kids to death or constantly telling them stuff. It's about actual conversations, ones where they get to tell you what *they* think. It's about cultivating an environment where they feel safe to talk to you.

Parent after parent thinks they are a safe place for their kids to share their hearts. Yet when the kid does, the parent goes into lecture mode. Or, worse, talks about their kid's stuff with other people. Safety is blown and the kid stops talking. Sometimes cultivating a conversational environment means simply keeping your mouth shut and listening or asking relevant questions that show interest. But be trustworthy with the treasures they bestow upon you.

Often we find that conversation success is tied to the right environment. Study your kids. Know the circumstances that lead them to open up a little. For a lot of kids, the best info is unloaded while they're eating. It's a good distraction and often fosters open conversation with less awkwardness than a face-to-face conversation. That's one reason dinnertime is so important.

In the Stanley house, once again, the approach was different for each child. If we wanted to chat with Andrew, all it took was sitting down with him and watching a Braves game or some other sport. If we had a little patience, he would start conversations pretty quickly.

Garrett opened up at night before bed. If I sat on the edge of his bed and scratched his back, he would talk as long as I would scratch. And I was willing to get a wrist cramp for it. No pain, no gain.

Allie wanted to unload the details of her day, but only right when she walked in the door from school. She would burst in with, "*Mom*, you won't believe . . ." Let me tell you something, I was right there waiting most days because I knew that if I missed that moment, she'd get busy with something else and I'd miss out. And I did *not* want to miss out.

When it came to harder conversations, Andy was great with Allie. She had a keyboard right beside her bed in her room. After Allie was tucked in, Andy would sit at the keyboard and play and sing Elton John or Taylor Swift songs. He had studied his daughter and knew exactly what she liked. After a couple of songs, they would chat and she'd usually open right up. I tended to be more effective in hard conversations with Garrett. Again, the back scratch thing. And Andrew, Mr. Gimme the Facts, could receive instruction and correction in a straightforward way from either of us.

Be a student of your kids. Figure out the best approaches based on their unique personalities, temperaments, and quirks.

A word of warning: If you get this conversation stuff right, your kids *will* talk to you. You might hear some shocking things. You'll need to work on your poker face. Really.

Stand in front of the mirror and practice, because it's coming for you.

Shaunti Feldhahn gives some great advice in her *For Parents Only* book: Don't freak out. Whatever you do, don't freak out in front of your teenager. And their definition of "freaking out" is *any* strong emotion. So dial it back.

When they tell you the crazy thing their friend did last weekend, *don't freak out*. When they share about the car accident they almost had on the way to school, *don't freak out*. When they tell you about the A they got in chemistry, be happy, yes, but *don't freak out*. Don't be the parent who cheers excessively in the bleachers at their game either. That's freaking out. We moms tend to freak out over the good stuff more than dads do. Don't do that.

It can be a delicate dance, this not freaking out thing, because we want to celebrate our kids. So what's a parent to do? We had a "celebrate plate," a dinner plate that had confetti painted all over it and the word *Celebrate* in large and colorful letters. It allowed us to be chill and let the plate do the "freaking out" for us. Instead of going crazy when a good thing happened, we would be appropriately excited, based on the varying degrees of excitement each kid liked, and I always tried to remember the celebrate plate at dinnertime.

Even when they made fun of it in high school, I'm pretty sure they still liked it. It wasn't over the top but made them feel noticed and celebrated. And everyone likes to be noticed and celebrated every once in a while.

Just remember, the fastest way to shut down a teenager is

to overemote. Practice that poker face. Calmly ask questions that keep them talking and engaged, but don't freak out. Use a posture that communicates, "Oh, really? Tell me more." You can circle back later for correction or clarification, but in the moment, it's most important to keep 'em talking.

Our kids told us stuff we never would have dreamed of telling our own parents. Sometimes when one of the kids revealed something, Andy and I would cut our eyes at each other, communicating silently, "Can you believe he just told us that?" And later one of us would ask the other, "Would you have ever told your parents that?"

Sometimes cultivating conversation is as simple as pressing pause on our emotions and forcing ourselves to respond rather than react. Save the reactions for later with your spouse or when you can scream into *your* pillow.

The second thing we discovered that boosts connecting over correcting boils down to a sentence we had to say out loud to ourselves from time to time.

Don't bail; let 'em fail.

Gosh, this was hard for me. I'm a natural-born fixer. And also a bailer. And I really love math. Combine those three characteristics, and you have a perfect storm brewing. I can't tell you how much math homework I did. Most afternoons, our foster daughter would sit beside me, playing on her phone, while I solved for *x*. It was a great system. Until test time.

Bailing out our kids hurts way more than it helps.

Swooping in and keeping them from failing may feel good in the moment, but they suffer later. And fall harder.

This is another of those scenarios where letting them suffer while the stakes are lower yields a better return. They learn lessons while the consequences are manageable. They develop skills and build muscle for better decision-making later, when the consequences of failure can be life-altering.

A girlfriend of mine was masterful at this. Her kids went to a private school pretty far from their house. They learned to get all their school stuff, projects, and homework papers gathered and in order the night before. Why? Because if they left anything behind, Mom wasn't delivering forgotten items to school later in the day, even when she really, really wanted to bail them out. The result? After one or two times of forgetting, the lesson was learned. Fast-forward about ten years, and these are three of the most responsible and resourceful young adults I know! I'm sure it isn't simply because they didn't go back for stuff or have their forgotten items delivered to them, but her refusal to bail them out certainly trained them to think and plan ahead.

The truth is, we *must* allow our kids to experience the natural consequences that stem from their actions. That's real life. That's how they learn most effectively. We all know an adult or two whose parents constantly bailed them out of trouble. Now they limp along in life, unable to fully function. It's sad to watch.

In my neighborhood growing up, there was a couple who married later in life. Let's call them Steve and Monica. Steve had been married before and had two amazing sons who were close to my age and nearing high school. Even though this couple was a bit older, they decided to expand their family. A third son was born (Monica's first). We'll call him Trey. To say Monica was overprotective would be an understatement. She constantly coddled Trey and excused every poor behavior with, "Oh, he's so tired," or "Well, that wasn't his fault because . . ."

Her coddling followed him into his school years, with Monica being every teacher's worst nightmare. A bad grade? She marched down to the school to explain why Trey deserved a higher score. A fight on the playground? "Not his fault. That Anderson kid has always been a problem." Science fair project? No third grader had ever created such a detailed report on the pH levels in the local soil.

Monica was a helicopter mom before we had a name for it. The older Trey got, the worse his offenses became. But Monica and Steve never let Trey experience the consequences of his behavior. By high school they were running interference between him and the law. Then when he was twenty-one, the offense included selling drugs in a high school parking lot to kids who couldn't even drive yet. That one left a mark.

Here's what I learned: Providing a buffer between our kids and the natural consequences they should experience is a gross disservice to them. Don't go rushing to the school with every forgotten assignment or lunch. Don't have a "conversation" with the parent of the kid your kid had a run-in with. Let them start figuring that stuff out. Guide them, encourage them, and even comfort them through it. But don't deprive them of their chances to learn from their mistakes.

The third contributing factor to connection with our kids is a big one:

Get interested in what interests them.

My parents are the best at this. They're in their eighties now and have not stopped. They do it with all of us, even the grandkids.

They hit the road and travel wherever necessary to put their eyes on the dorm rooms, first homes, and apartments of their kids and grandkids because they like to visualize them where they live. They've put thousands of miles on their cars to get to baseball games, dance recitals, and graduations. They keep up with technology so they can email, text, and follow their people on social media.

One of my favorite examples was a photo and text I received from my dad's administrative assistant. She sent a pic of Dad sitting on top of his desk, staring at his iPhone. The text said, "Your dad just said, 'My notifications are not coming through, and I think I'm missing stuff.'" She followed this with the laughing face emoji. I sent approximately twelve back.

Andy is also great at getting involved in our kids' activities. He is very open about his lack of interest in sports, but when our boys hit the sports-playing years, he dove in. He learned all the rules and coached as many seasons as he could of whatever sports they played. And he was great at it because he's a master at strategy. A few years into Little League, other coaches were fighting to coach alongside him. (He won't admit that, but I was there and I know it's true. So whatever.)

Parents often fall into the trap of trying to get their kids to follow *their* interests rather than encouraging them to develop their own. Growing up, I was a gymnast. I was decent and I loved it. So, naturally, when Allie was about five or six, I signed her up. I didn't just sign her up, though. I researched the best gym for beginner gymnasts who had Olympic potential. I bought her all the leotards. She likes sparkle; I like serious. So we compromised on a little bit of sparkle, but not so much that she wouldn't be taken seriously.

The gym I chose was run by two former Olympians who had been coached by Bela Karolyi and Nadia Comaneci, my childhood *idol*. The gym had an observation balcony for parents. So this would do nicely.

What I didn't anticipate was Allie hating it. She liked the leotards, the mini trampoline, and being barefoot on the squishy mats but didn't like the stern coaches, the sweating, the balance beam, the backbends, or anything else.

I'll never forget sitting up in the observation area with the boys. Andrew turned to me and said, "Mom, I think we need to keep looking for Allie's thing." Absolutely not. We love this. This is going to be great when she gets the hang of it. Right? No, not right.

I had to come to terms with the fact that this was Allie,

not me. It was worth finding the activities *she* loved. She was great at tons of things, not only one. She's artsy and creative and loved horses and painting and writing and communicating. She's amazing, and I'm so glad we let her find *her* things.

Dads can be especially vulnerable to the temptation of forcing their own interests on their kids. We've all seen the dad-coach who loses it in the dugout when his son strikes out. Or the one who has dreams of NFL stardom for his son since he couldn't make good on the dream himself. Or the parents who push their daughter on the track to beat her last time, when all she wants is to write in her journal and dream of her someday bestselling novel.

Think of all that's missed when we try to push our agendas on our kids rather than helping them develop their own. A felt rejection creeps into our kids' hearts and minds when they're convinced they don't measure up to those parental expectations. It's damaging, and it'll be a prime culprit in keeping our kids from wanting to come home when they no longer have to.

Figure out what lights up your kids. Learn it. Encourage it. Invest in it. You'll be so glad you did. And it might just be the thing that launches them into a forever hobby or even a career.

So cultivate constant conversations. Don't bail; let 'em fail. And get interested in the things that interest them. This is connecting and setting them up to succeed.

And that brings us to the friendship years.

The Friendship Years (18+ Years Old)

May I just say? Empty-nester-hood is amazing! We're thriving here. We loved our years of parenting. Mostly. And we're loving this season. We're together *a lot*. More on all of that in the marriage chapter.

But this is where Andy and I are now—the friendship years with our kids. It's new. It's amazing. If we didn't know our kids and we met them, we'd want to be friends with them. They're fun and funny, and they like each other and us. They seem to love coming home. That's exactly what we decided to shoot for on that drive to Hilton Head three decades ago. And we're seeing it pay off.

Not long ago, a few folks from our church team took our three kids to dinner, without their spouses and without us. The purpose was to mine stories from them to use for video content to go along with this book and to get their perspective on some of the content we're using in these chapters. Maybe to be sure we're not making stuff up? I'm not sure.

Within twenty-four hours Andy and I heard from all three kids about how it went. After dinner the church team headed home to their families. Andrew, Garrett, and Allie stood outside the restaurant and decided they weren't ready to part ways. They walked down the street to a café to hang out some more. They laughed and talked and just generally enjoyed hanging out together and catching up.

They each, in their own way, communicated to us how

life-giving that time was. And each was determined to have these sibling get-togethers more often.

Andy and I shed tears of joy listening to each of them talk about it. It was the deepest kind of joy—seeing our kids love each other and *choose* each other. Because, let me tell you, they haven't always. They got on each other's nerves aplenty. Growing up, they preferred friends over sibs for sure. They didn't let each other into their rooms, and they gave each other the silent treatment all the time. At times, I wondered if they would ever be friends. Yet here we are. And I'm a grateful mama.

Gathering regularly around the dinner table is still common for us. All three kids live in the Atlanta area, so at least once a month we have family dinner night, sometimes at a restaurant and sometimes here at home. Sometimes the celebrate plate comes out, but freaking out isn't taboo anymore. I can let my giddiness out if I want to, and they just roll their eyes and pretend not to like it.

Andy and I are convinced that tailoring our parenting strategies to the four stages of parenting is part of why we're reaping some benefits now. Certainly there are other variables that sink or sail the ship, and there's no magic formula for ending up with kids you like. But for us, with other variables relatively steady, deep and authentic friendship came on the heels of disciplining during the discipline years, training during the training years, and coaching during the coaching years. We appropriately loosened the tethers along the way.

Even so, as any parent with grown children will tell you, parenting never ends. We continue to have opinions about what our kids should and shouldn't do, who they should date and marry, how they should raise their kids, and on and on it goes.

We should never stop thinking about our approach to parenting based on all the factors: individual personalities, specific temperaments, degrees of openness to input, and more. But sometimes we have to dive in and say something. None of us want to see our child crash and burn, and wonder if speaking up would've made a difference. At the same time, unsolicited advice to adult children often feels like criticism. Once again, approach is everything. Here is a great illustration of choosing the right approach. I'll let Andy tell it since he's the one who heard it first.

My job in student ministry allowed me to get to know parents of middle and high school students who had great relationships with their kids. One dad in particular told me a story that had a huge impact on my own parenting. His son, Don, was about to graduate from high school and head off to the University of Georgia.

Like many high school seniors, Don had no idea what he wanted to be when he grew up. So his dad said, "Don, whatever you want to do with your life, I'll support and use whatever influence I have to help. But until you know, will you trust me to point you in the direction I think is best? The moment you figure out what you want to do, if you decide to move in a different direction, I'm in." Don agreed to the plan. Now, that Don would take that kind of advice from his dad said a lot about their relationship up to that point.

The dad suggested that Don major in business and plan to go to law school. Based on Don's aptitude and personality, his dad thought he should at least move in that direction. So that's what Don did. And when he finished college, he went to law school. To this day, Don is practicing law and thriving. His dad was able to see something Don couldn't see at that time. His dad knew he needed to say something, but he also knew approach was everything. So he asked permission to give counsel, rather than offering it unsolicited.

"Until you know, will you trust me to give you some direction?" This was brilliant. And twenty years later, I brought it back.

Andrew was about to head off to college with no idea what he wanted to major in. So I gave him the same speech as that father. "Andrew, will you allow me to point you in a direction until you decide what you want to do?" "Sure, Dad." I suggested he get a finance degree. Based on his aptitude, but not necessarily his interests at the time, I knew finance would likely be a good fit. And it would set him up for a variety of opportunities. But I assured him, "If you change your mind, discover something else, no problem." Andrew ended up sticking with finance all the way through college, and he landed a great job right out of school.

And then he started going to comedy clubs after work, doing stand-up for twenty dollars and a burger. After a couple of years of that, he and I had "the talk" (not that talk). "Dad, I like my job, but I want to quit and do stand-up comedy full-time." He had hit the tipping point where he was making as much money doing stand-up as he was with his finance job. But economizing days off and doing the late-night comedy scene made the day job rough.

"Andrew, I did not pay out-of-state tuition for four years so you could throw it all away on some harebrained idea that won't pay the bills. Besides, what are people going to think when they find out my son . . ." Nope. That's not what I said.

My responsibility as a dad isn't to decide what he does with his life. My responsibility is to put my weight behind what he decides to do with his life. It's his life. Besides, that was the deal. And honestly, it was easy for me and for Sandra. That's the way we'd been parenting all along. We had ramped up to it during those coaching years.

Andy's right. We had ramped up to it. But sometimes we still get it wrong. We've all been there. We see something, and we think we need to speak up. So we dive right in without carefully considering our approach. Again, this is a Sandra problem, not an Andy problem. He always takes time to think. I need to check it off my list. Also, I think if I don't say something now, time will go by and I might miss the opportunity. What in the world will they do if they miss my extraordinary insight, advice, and correction? I have so much good information. I'm sure that's what they need: information.

One day Allie and I were in the car together. I have no idea where we were going, but I do know it was after high school, well into the friendship years. She asked a question, and I launched into sharing the vast information held in my vault. She was quiet for a few minutes, then said, "Mom, sometimes I hesitate to share something or ask a question because you tend to tell me *way* more than I asked." She was respectful and careful in *her* approach. But she knew I needed to know. She knew that I treasure our relationship, and she also knew this tendency of mine would ultimately impede what's most important to both of us—our friendship. I was so thankful she told me.

Here's one more story, one that encouraged Andy and me that maybe we had accomplished the "want to come home even when they don't have to" goal. The spring of 2016 rolled around, and it was time to think about the annual Hilton Head trip with my entire family—eighteen of us. Andy and I decided it might be nice to go early and enjoy a few days of quiet before everyone else arrived. We both had writing projects to work on. I was in seminary and a new semester would be cranking up on the front end of vacation, so this extra time would be perfect.

We let our kids know our plans and that we'd see them when they arrived for the regular week. Then Garrett and Danielle, who had not started their postgraduation jobs, asked if they could come early with us. Andy and I looked at each other and grinned. We knew that not all college seniors would want a beach trip with parents.

I get what you might be thinking. "Who wouldn't want a free chunk of days on Hilton Head Island? This doesn't prove a thing." You're not wrong. But there's a flip side to this whole "kids who want to be with us" thing. *We wanted to be with them too.* Even though we had planned to have a quiet few days before the rest of the Stanley/Walker/Holley clan arrived, we loved that they wanted to come because we like them, *and* they seem to like us. And, by golly, *that* was the goal all along.

CHAPTER 4

Don't Worship the Devil

(SANDRA)

Growing up, we didn't have a lot of rules in our home. My older sister, younger brother, and I didn't need many rules. Not because we were better-than-average children. We weren't. We didn't need a lot of rules because my dad had *a look* that kept us all in line.

Allow me to introduce you to Lieutenant Colonel Robert Walker, USMC.

My father didn't begin our day with push-ups, but he did begin it early. And he began it by asking for our plans. Nearly every morning before school, he would drop by our bedrooms and ask in a half-teasing drill sergeant voice, "What are you gonna accomplish today?" If we didn't have an answer, we made one up on the spot. Occasionally I would respond, "Probably watch TV all day, Pop." We would laugh because we both knew better.

My dad expected a lot of us, but we knew he was in it with us. In spite of his Marine/Eagle Scout/entrepreneur exterior, there was never any doubt that he loved his kids. When we made up our minds to pursue something, he was all in. When I became interested in gymnastics, he built me a balance beam in the backyard. When my sister decided she wanted to be a nurse, he got to work finding the best nursing schools.

When we left home for college, he carried a three-by-five card in his shirt pocket with each of our schedules on it—not because he wanted to check on us but because he was genuinely interested in what we were doing. If something was interesting to us, it was interesting to him.

When my brother showed interest in acting, something my dad had no category in his brain for, he supported my brother's decision to move to California for a season. And, in true Bob Walker fashion, when Dad visited and saw the neighborhood my brother lived in, he started sending money to a homeless gentleman in the area to keep an eye on my brother. True story.

So while Dad had high expectations, he never imposed his will. While he had a plan for each of our lives, he remained open-handed. Perhaps the best illustration of his rigid flexibility is when I told him about Andy. I was finishing up my junior year at Georgia Tech, my dad's alma mater. He had already begun preparation for my next step, an internship with a US senator in Washington, DC. So when I told him I was dating a youth pastor who worked for his dad at a Baptist church, well, you can imagine. My grandmother, in contrast, was thrilled. She watched Andy's dad on television every Sunday morning. When Dad met Andy and realized we were serious, he scrapped his ambitious political plans for me and embraced my future as the wife of a Baptist youth pastor. And he tried really hard to be happy for me.

Speaking of Andy . . .

Andy didn't grow up with many rules either. In the ways that matter most, the atmosphere and expectations in his home were similar to those in mine. Our fathers, both of whose biological fathers died when they were young, shared a similar value system, a value system that could be summarized in one word. And that one word shaped the way we raised our children as well. That word? *Honor.*

Like our families before us, Andy and I didn't create many rules in our home. We had only two hard-and-fast rules, two nonnegotiables. These were Andy's idea, and I am most grateful.

1. Honor your mother.
2. Don't tell a lie.

I particularly like the first one, for obvious reasons, so let's start there.

While I'm sure the centrality of honor doesn't come as a surprise, you may wonder, "Why just Mom? Why not honor everybody?" I wondered the same thing at first. But Andy decided honoring me was a keystone rule.

Maybe you're familiar with the concept of a keystone

habit. In his book *The Power of Habit*, Charles Duhigg describes keystone habits as small behaviors with large ripple effects. A keystone habit has a cascading effect. It sparks a chain reaction of other positive habits. For example, exercise is a keystone habit. The rhythm of an exercise routine creates other routines as well. People who exercise regularly are more prone to make healthy food choices. And getting up early to exercise requires going to bed earlier, which results in a better night's sleep, which impacts productivity, which affects self-esteem. And on and on it goes.

A keystone rule works the same way. It has a cascading, or trickle-down, effect. Honoring Mom cascaded to honoring Andy because he was the one who required it to begin with. Learning to honor one person set an expectation for how the kids were to honor each other as well as other adults. Honoring Mom required prioritizing what was important to Mom: a clean room, a made bed, a respectful tone.

This one rule saved us from having to make a bunch of other rules. And—this is important—it provided us with a relational *why* behind the *what*. We didn't require our kids to make their beds because it was some sort of moral imperative handed down from above. It was a demonstration of respect for their mom. Again, it trickled down. Granted, sometimes we had to help it trickle down, but we didn't have to spend a lot of time making up reasons for why.

Here's an example.

Like most kids, when ours were young, they would sometimes leave a wet towel on the floor or, worse, on a bed. There

are several ways to address this common domestic dilemma.
Here's how Andy handled it. He connected the dots between
the behavior and our honor mandate.

One summer afternoon, he walked into one of our adorable
children's rooms and noticed some clothes tossed about on the
floor along with a couple of wet towels that had come home
from the pool. Instead of picking them up, he called for said
adorable child to come upstairs. As soon as he saw the mess,
he started cleaning up. Andy stopped him and said, "No. I'm
going to do it. But I need you to ask me to do it. I need you
to say, 'Dad, will you please pick up my clothes and put my
towels in the bathroom?'" Our adorable son was horrified.
"I'll do it, Dad." Andy insisted, "No, I'm going to do it, but I
need you to ask me to." For a minute there was a standoff, and
then Andy explained: "When you leave clothes on the floor,
you are basically asking me or your mom to clean up after you.
So go ahead and ask me." By this time the adorable child was
irritated and insisted on doing it himself. But Andy held firm.
He stood there until the child finally muttered, "Dad, will you
please pick up my towels and clothes?" Andy got to work.
"Dad, can I at least help?" "Nope. This is what Mom has to
do when you aren't here." It was so uncomfortable because
it felt super dishonoring. Because it was. And this adorable
kiddo knew it.

In our experience, once our kids understood what
it meant to honor Mom, we didn't have to explicitly state
much else. Honoring the people Mom honored was a way of
honoring Mom.

Another way to honor Mom was to be nice to each other so Mom didn't always have to step in to sort out sibling conflicts. Rather than make a rule for each of these behaviors, we focused on *Honor your mother.* Getting that keystone habit right meant that a long list of other desired behaviors followed. That said, it didn't happen without frequent nudging along the way.

If you ask Andy how he came up with this idea, he will be quick to give his dad the credit. He taught Andy from a young age that the way he treated his mom would establish a pattern for how he would eventually treat his wife. His dad understood the generational implications of how a young man treats his mother. I've told Charles on multiple occasions how grateful I am that he raised Andy to honor his mother. And I'm sure the fact that both of our fathers were raised primarily by their moms played into this as well. Like Andy's dad, my dad had little to no tolerance for disrespectful language or behavior toward our mom.

That one keystone rule cascaded into a second and now a third generation as we watch our married son, Garrett, honor his wife, Danielle. This was also the source of the high expectations Allie had while dating, which led her to Clay, her amazing husband.

And then there is the text Andy and I received.

Andrew had recently gotten engaged to a fabulous young lady. From the outset of the relationship, his girlfriend was impressed with how well he treated her. One day she asked, "Andrew, you've never had a serious girlfriend. How is it that you know how to treat me so well?" His simple and immediate response? "I've watched my dad treat my mom this way my whole life." She immediately texted the story to Andy and me. We cried a little. Okay, maybe a lot.

The power of the keystone honor rule continues to cascade into my experience with my children today. As we will discuss later, the ultimate win in parenting is a mutually satisfying relationship with our adult children. Insisting on honor in the early years lays the groundwork for that relationship.

Here's one more example of how this rule played out in our home. You'll definitely want to steal this one.

Dinnertime is perhaps the most important event of the day for a family. It can also be one of the most chaotic, especially for moms if they're the ones carrying the weight of getting dinner on the table. Early on, Andy insisted that our kids not eat until I was seated and we had asked the blessing. But that was challenging, especially with hungry boys and food on the table. Not to be deterred, Andy took it up a notch and required our boys to stand behind their chairs until Allie and I were both seated. And then no one started eating until I was ready or gave the go-ahead. If that sounds over the top, well, try it before you judge us.

Waiting for me to be seated first was, and continues to be, a practical and visual way of honoring me. They deferred. They put me first. Not to mention I may have earned a bit of deferential treatment considering how long it took to prepare dinner compared with how quickly they devoured it.

This discipline also had an unexpected benefit. The kids were more prone to ask how they could help, primarily in an attempt to get the party started, but we'll pretend it was pure thoughtfulness. And it gave everyone a moment or two while standing to notice the time and effort I put into creating their meal. I felt appreciated. Honored.

And so did Allie.

Imagine how powerful it was for our teenage daughter to see her dad and brothers standing—hundreds of times through the years—out of respect for her. It set the bar high for the way she would expect men to treat her, which is exactly what Andy and I intended. We wanted her to be so accustomed to being honored and shown deference that she'd be uncomfortable with anything less. My mom heart is so happy that her dad and brothers made this incredible investment in her future. What a gift. And it was as easy as standing up.

So while *Honor your mother* may have begun with me as the focus, it cascaded into our kids' relationships with each other—and with those outside the family.

When Andrew and Garrett had friends over for dinner, their friends would inevitably plop themselves down at the table as soon as dinner was announced. Before long they would realize they were the only ones seated and would get back up and stand behind their chairs as well—with no clue why! Once I was seated and everybody sat down, they would follow suit. Eventually we had our kids' friends trained as well.

From Andy:

Before Sandra moves on, I want to jump in with an additional comment for my fellow fathers. There is another, though often delayed, benefit to the *honor your mother* rule.

Dads, if you teach your children to honor their mother, and they see *you* honor their mother, they will instinctively honor you as well.

Ultimately they will honor you for requiring them to honor her. Aim for one and you'll get both. What's more, when you point out how your kids' behavior misses the mark, they will see you *defending someone's honor* rather than merely *requiring obedience* for obedience's or compliance's sake.

Honor their mother with your words, tone, and behavior and your kids will return the favor.

As wonderful as the preceding paragraphs make all this sound, honoring others did not always go smoothly.

Why?

Because honor does not come naturally. It must be *learned*. Selfishness comes naturally. And that must be *tamed*. In chapter 5, Andy will describe two situations where our boys all but abandoned honor. And he'll detail our response. But as you'll discover, having a north star of honoring others—and honoring your mother in particular—will provide you with something specific and relational by which to set your parenting course, something by which to navigate the choppy and sometimes turbulent seas of parenting.

So that's rule number one: Honor your mother.

Our second nonnegotiable was *Don't tell a lie.*

But we didn't articulate it that way. What we said was, "The worst thing you can do is tell a lie." They must have heard it a thousand times. "The worst thing you can do is tell a lie. The worst thing you can do is tell a lie. The worst thing you can do . . ." And we know they got the message. I'll let Andy tell this one.

When Andrew was around six years old, he and I were driving somewhere. He was in the back seat. And he was especially quiet, which meant he was thinking. He's definitely the thinker. Suddenly, with no setup, he blurted, "Dad, I know something worse than telling a lie." He had heard our "There's nothing worse . . ." line so many times, apparently he took it as a challenge. Surely there was something worse than telling a lie. And he had finally discovered what that something was.

"Really, Andrew? What's worse than telling a lie?"

"Worshiping the devil."

He had me. And for a moment I considered adding a third rule:

1. Honor your mother.
2. Don't tell a lie.
3. Don't worship the devil.

But since there was no indication of devil worship

in our home, I stuck with two rules. But I kept my eyes open.

Back to Sandra.

So, you ask, why lying? Of all the offenses out there, why choose this one?

The reason lying made our top-two list is that *lying breaks a relationship*. That's the "why" we attached to this rule from the beginning. We didn't cite it as one of the Ten Commandments. We didn't front-load it with, "The Bible says . . ." It's simple. Lying breaks a relationship, and we didn't want our relationships with our children broken.

That was reason enough. But there *is* another angle. Lying *dishonors* the person being lied to. In both instances, the relationship is in jeopardy.

We taught our kids that when you can't believe what you hear from another person, everything is off balance. The relationship is damaged.

- How can I trust you this time if you lied last time?
- How can I take your word for it if you don't always stick to your word?

Honesty is so foundational in relationships that Andy and I knew it had to be a nonnegotiable for our family. We could correct bad behavior. We could handle disrespect. But lying? There are no relational work-arounds for that. Lying signals an end to the relationship. It represents an impasse. Relationally speaking, it is the worst thing you can do. And, of course, the older a child is, the more skilled they become at it. So we addressed it early and often. "The worst thing you can do is tell a lie."

During the coaching years, when kids have more independence and freedom, if you can't trust that what they tell you is true, parenting becomes extremely complicated. Conversations about technology and social media and sleepovers and homework and borrowing the car—they're almost impossible to navigate if there's a chance your child is lying to you. For that reason, we tended to *overcorrect* when our kids didn't tell the truth. And we not only *disciplined* our children for *lying*. We also *trained* them to tell the *truth*.

There's a big difference. Let me explain.

Thanks to our years in student ministry, we were aware of something that most parents might not think about: incriminating oneself is not reflexive. It's not instinctive. Self-protection is instinctive. Nobody wants to look bad. We will do or say just about anything *not* to look bad.

Self-preservation and reputation preservation are hardwired into all of us, including your babies, your toddlers, and certainly your middle school– and high school–aged kids. So when telling the truth will cost your kids something, lying *feels right*. When telling the truth will make your children look bad, feel bad, or experience something bad, it does not come naturally. So children must be taught, not simply expected, to tell the truth. It requires coaching. And the earlier you begin, the better.

When the kids were young, we did something we found

super effective. Anytime we asked one of our children a question that we thought they may not want to answer truthfully, we would preface the question by saying, "I'm going to ask you something, and you may be tempted to lie. I really don't want you to lie to me. Our relationship is too important for that. Ready?"

In many instances, children lie because they're caught off guard. Adults too, actually. And if we're angry when we confront our kids, our body language and tone automatically force them into self-preservation mode. What do *you* do when you are in self-preservation mode? You instinctively, reactively, reflexively preserve yourself. What do you do when you feel like you're being threatened or attacked? You defend yourself. Lying is generally a means of self-defense.

This approach was very effective. And it honored our children. It prepared them to tell the truth. It gave them space to collect their thoughts and *decide* rather than *react*. This approach set them up to succeed, to act courageously. The confrontation took place with the goal of preserving the relationship, not simply trying to get to the bottom of whatever happened. Besides, when our kids are young, we usually already know what happened. But we need them to own it.

Honesty is a muscle. Muscles get stronger with use. The more you coax your children to tell the truth when they're young, the less you'll have to threaten them when they're older. Double down during the discipline and training years. Make it unacceptable to lie, and enthusiastically reward the truth. When your toddlers become teens, you'll be glad you did.

Those were our two long-standing rules. One *do* and one *don't*. For all the years we had our children and our foster children living with us, those two covered just about every transgression that needed addressing. More importantly, those two rules underscored and reinforced what was most important to us: mutually satisfying relationships.

As you may have already discovered, if you have a lot of rules in your home, you will eventually end up punishing yourself. Worse, eventually you'll be inconsistent in your application and your kids *will* call you on it. So keep it simple. Keep it relational. And on those occasions when correction is necessary? Well, I'll let Andy pick it up there.

CHAPTER 5

Designer Consequences

(ANDY)

One of Sandra's most brilliant moments of parenting came when the boys were eight and ten years old. She and I went out for the evening, and our longtime babysitter Pam looked after the kids.

When we walked through the door at the end of the night, we followed the usual script, asking her, "How'd it go? Was everyone well behaved?" Typically, Pam cheerfully reported that everything had been great. This time, however, she said, "Well, the boys . . ." She was reluctant to fill in the details of their misdeeds but eventually did. And it wasn't good. They had been extremely disrespectful to her.

The next morning, they knew they were busted when Sandra woke them up earlier than normal and sent them straight to their desks to write apology notes. We were homeschooling at the time. Well, Sandra was. Once she deemed their phonetic spelling good enough, she said, "Get dressed in your nice clothes, get all the money out of your spending jars, and meet me in the car." The boys had no idea what was going on. But they knew this was big. Side note: They were just old enough to appreciate money and just young enough not to have much of it.

After everybody was buckled in, Sandra laid out the game plan. First, they would head to the grocery store where the boys would each buy Pam flowers with their own money. Then they would drive to Pam's office, deliver the flowers and notes, and apologize in person for their behavior the night before.

They were horrified.

I wasn't there to see it, but I know for certain that as the boys walked past all of Pam's colleagues on the way to her desk, they were wishing we had taken away every privilege and every toy and canceled Christmas instead of subjecting them to this. They would have given up everything to avoid this consequence.

As I said, it was brilliant. Brilliant and oh so effective.

I begin this chapter with this story because it perfectly illustrates what we came to believe early on was the most effective way to approach and employ discipline. For the remainder of this chapter, I'll explain why this approach is so effective, as well as unpack what the preceding illustration demonstrates.

Let's start with the basic question: What's the point?

Why do we discipline our children? What are we trying

to accomplish? Maybe you've never stopped to think about it. I'm convinced most parents haven't. When your child misbehaves, you react. You put them in time-out. You send them to their room. You take away their phone. You probably do or say what your parents did or said to you. Or perhaps the pendulum has swung the other way and you intentionally don't discipline your kids the way your parents did. That's not a discipline goal. That's a *not* goal. *I'm not going to discipline like my parents!* But even that doesn't answer the question of why you discipline at all. Either way, you are in the majority because most parents never establish or identify a goal when it comes to discipline. And if there is no preestablished goal, there is rarely any discipline. Punishment, yes. Payback, yes. Teach 'em a lesson! Maybe. But what's the lesson? Don't get caught next time?

Punishment is not discipline. Punishment is punishment.

Discipline makes a person better. Punishment rarely makes anybody better. It simply makes them more careful. And perhaps bitter. Not better. The message of punishment is this: *If you don't obey me, bad things will happen to you. If you inconvenience or embarrass me, I'll inconvenience or embarrass you.* There's rarely any positive or permanent change, other than to the relationship. More on that later.

Fortunately, there's a better way.

When honoring others is the chief value in a family (as we've argued it should be), disobedience, dishonesty, and disrespect are problematic because they dishonor another person. They damage a relationship. Or, to put it another way, at the heart of every transgression is a *someone*, not a *something*.

The goal of discipline is to teach your child how to restore the relationship they damaged.

This is what Sandra got so right in the way she handled the boys' behavior toward Pam. Taking away their LEGOs or making them do extra chores would have been pointless punishment. Pam's feelings still would have been hurt, and the boys only would have learned to dial it back a bit next time. Instead, Sandra walked them through the steps of making things right in the relationship.

This is a skill that has to be taught. You teach your children to use a fork. You teach them to tie their shoes. And you have to teach your children how to restore a relationship. You've met plenty of adults who can eat with a fork and tie their shoes but who never learned to restore a broken relationship. They never learned because no one ever taught them, and perhaps they never saw it modeled either.

So they say things like, "I don't know why you're still upset. I said I was sorry!" No one ever taught them that an apology alone doesn't rebuild a relationship. In some cases, an apology alone makes it worse. We should discipline with the goal of teaching our children the critical life skill of making things right with the people they've wronged. Your child's future spouse, colleagues, and friends will be glad you did. Your grandchildren will be glad you did.

Effective discipline requires two things from your child—confession and restitution. And it requires two words from you—*Oh no!* Let me explain those first.

When your child misbehaves, what's your typical reaction? When they break a rule or act out or mouth off, what is generally the first thing you say?

"No!"

"You know better . . ."

"How many times have I told you . . . ?"

The problem with the natural, go-to responses—or reactions—is that they put you and your child on opposing teams. Even if the transgression wasn't aimed at you, a typical reaction sets you up as the offended party. It appears as if, and feels to your child as if, your relationship with your child is in jeopardy. You've become an adversary. I'm sure as a teenager you remember feeling like your parents couldn't wait to catch you doing something wrong so they could punish you. If you're not careful, your approach to discipline will create that assumption. It will pit you and your child against each other.

A better posture to take when your kid misbehaves is, *Oh no!*

Oh no! is siding with your child against their disobedience. It's *Oh no! We—you and I—are so sorry you did that because now you'll have to face the consequences. Oh no! I am for you, and I hate that you are going to be penalized for your behavior.*

An *Oh no!* reaction keeps you and your child on the same team relationally. They aren't off the hook, but you aren't the bad guy. You are just as sad as they are and for the same reason.

Well, maybe not *just* as sad.

My dad was great at responding this way. I got my first traffic ticket driving home from school in my mom's beige four-door Catalina. It was a spectacularly unimpressive vehicle. I remember walking through the door of our house, so afraid to tell him. When I did, he certainly wasn't happy. But his posture wasn't one of outrage. It was *Oh no! That's too bad. I hate that for you. Because* you *have to deal with the consequences.* He asked, "So what's next?" I was a teenager. I didn't know what was next. In the eleventh grade, I didn't know much of anything. He told me that the instructions for what to do next were on the back of the ticket. He didn't launch into a lecture or make it an issue between the two of us. He sided *with* me *against* the offense. And a month later when I had to go to court, he was there next to me.

Beyond protecting your relationship with your child, *Oh no!* has a practical benefit too. It buys you time. When your kids are young, an instant response to disobedience or disrespect is appropriate. You have to connect the dots quickly. If you wait too long to discipline a toddler, they won't make the connection. But the older your child, the longer you can—and should—wait to decide how they must make up for their misdeed.

Why? Well, for starters, it gives you time to calm down and think creatively. That's right . . . creatively. When you're angry, you're not creative. You're angry! So you reach for what is close by and familiar. You end up punishing your kids the same way every time regardless of the offense. That's not discipline.

Another reason waiting is good is that it reflects real life. In the justice system, when someone commits a crime, it might be a year before they go to trial. But most importantly, waiting communicates to your child that you weren't expecting them to do what they did. *You did what? Oh no! I'm so surprised. You called your sister what? Oh no! I'm shocked!*

Generally, one of the first questions out of a child's mouth when they know they're busted is, "What are you gonna do?" Kids want to know their fate. Immediately. How much is this going to cost them? When you employ this approach, you shrug and say, "I don't know. I wasn't expecting this. This took me totally by surprise. I have to think about it."

Now, this approach will not work if you regularly pre-assign a consequence to a rule violation. You know what I'm talking about: "If I come home and your room is still a mess, you'll have to . . ." "If you go into your sister's room again without asking, I will . . ." "You can go, but if you aren't home in time for dinner, you won't be leaving the house for the rest of the weekend."

If you're in the habit of preassigning consequences, please stop.

Preassigning a consequence sends the message, *Not only am I expecting you to mess up, I'm also prepared for it.* Worse, it robs your child of the opportunity to honor you by obeying without the threat of a consequence. If your son or daughter knows they are going to lose their driving privileges if they are late, you don't know, and they don't know, why they are racing to get home on time. Is it to avoid punishment, or is it to honor your request?

Getting your mind and heart to a place of *Oh no!* releases

the pressure valve for your emotions. Discipline is no longer fraught with conflict and hostility, which means you'll be in the right frame of mind for the fun part.

Yes, I mean it. What comes next can be fun. Do you believe me?

Pretend for a moment that you're the dad of a teenage son. Let's say one day your son ignores the number one house rule: Honor your mother. Imagine he is (hypothetically) sitting in the driver's seat of the car you allow him to drive, and while his mother is talking to him, he rolls up the car window in her face because he doesn't like what she is telling him, then backs out of the garage and drives off!

As the dad in that scenario, what do you do? Does *Oh no!* work in a situation like that?

Oh yes.

And this *Oh yes* is not hypothetical for Sandra and me. (Just so you know, I'm leaving out a few details to protect the guilty.) To say I was angry doesn't begin to describe how I felt. And like every parent of a teenager, I was tempted to start taking things away. What else can you do to a six-foot-one sixteen-year-old? But I managed to claw my way back to sanity and regain my *Oh no!* posture. He knew I knew, and he knew something was going to happen. Or not happen. When he got around to asking me what would happen, I acted shocked, hurt, and sad.

Acted.

It took me a few days to figure out what to do. Sandra began to wonder if I was going to do anything. She really was hurt. As I regained my emotional bearings, I was able to focus on the goal of discipline: relationship restoration. And trust me, the relationship needed some tender loving care.

I'll tell you what I settled on in a paragraph or two. You may want to borrow it sometime. But in light of our goal, I knew the consequence had to include the two steps necessary for getting any relationship back on the right track: confession and restitution.

From a young age, we taught our kids that a guilty conscience creates a relational wall. You've experienced this if you've ever been on the giving or receiving end of the silent treatment. That's a relational wall. The person who's been wronged feels mad. And the person who was wrong feels bad. Things in the relationship are unsettled. And they won't be right until the guilty party confesses and owns their slice of the conflict pie.

In light of that, when it comes to training our kids in the art of relationship restoration, the first step is to teach them how to apologize properly. As soon as your kids could talk, you probably taught them some form of an apology. If you're still in those training years, let me offer three quick tips.

Number one: Require your children to apologize in complete sentences. "Sorry" is not a complete sentence. "Sorry" is a sorry excuse for an apology. A good apology always includes a pronoun. "*I'm* sorry." Then they should name their offense with a verb. "I'm sorry I *lied* to you."

Number two: Your children should apologize to everyone affected by their actions. That means you, their siblings, their teachers, their friends, even their friends' parents.

Number three: Leverage the apology for maximum impact. Make it an event. Face-to-face. With eye contact. This is why we had our kids write apology letters and, when possible, hand-deliver their letters to the person they offended. This is one of several contexts in which sending a text may be woefully inadequate. Remember, the goal is restoration, so choose a medium accordingly.

Once an apology has been made, it's time for restitution. It can begin with the next thing out of their mouth. Teach your child to follow every apology with, "Is there anything I can do to make it up to you?" They are going to hate this. But it's important for kids to understand that when their behavior falls short, they've taken something away from the other person. That's why we say, "You *owe* them an apology." Restitution is the process of making up the honor they owe the other person.

Notice how different that process is from typical punishment. Unlike with punishment, there's no hint of payback—*You did something to me, so I'll do something to you*—which is important because *payback* doesn't bring the *relationship back*. This is why grounding your son or daughter or taking away their things rarely works long term. Forbidding video games for a week after your son hits his sister doesn't repair the relationship between the two of them. Not to mention, before long you'll run out of meaningful things to take away. In most cases taking things away has nothing to do with the offense.

So instead of punishing, pause, regain your balance, and discipline. Create a path to restoration and restitution.

Now—fair warning—as you've already picked up on, this approach requires more creativity, time, and involvement than taking stuff away or putting your child in time-out. But that should be expected, because the goal of discipline is not isolation. It's *re*lation. And relationships require time and involvement. It would have been much easier and certainly less time-consuming for Sandra to take away the boys' toys than it was for her to spend the morning taking them to buy flowers, driving to Pam's office, parking the car, locating her office, then returning home to a day that was already half shot. But all that extra effort was worth it. It will be worth it for you as well.

Here's why.

Chances are good that years from now your little boy or your middle school daughter will fall in love and get married. And when they hit one of those inevitable bumps in their relationship and communication breaks down, or perhaps a heart is broken, they either will or won't be prepared to restore the relationship. And that relationship will be almost as important to you as it is to them. What you do between now and when your child turns eighteen may determine whether they enter adulthood with the skill of restoring a relationship, a life skill far too many adults never fully develop. So this is a big deal. A big, often time-consuming deal. So start early and stick with it.

The importance of this skill is what I had in mind when I

made my way upstairs several days after the car window incident. As a result of his blatant disrespectful behavior toward his mother, I instructed my son to ask his mother out on a date. He would choose the restaurant. It had to be somewhere nice. He would drive and pay for dinner. No friends or siblings—just the two of them.

His eyes said, "You're kidding!"

His mouth said, "Yes, sir."

Sandra refers to this as my finest parenting moment.

When they walked through the door after their date, Sandra's eyes communicated, "Mission accomplished." The relationship was restored. There was no need for further discipline.

And speaking of Sandra . . .

Yes, I can't resist interrupting this story to add a bit of commentary. When Andy told me to expect an invitation from our son for dinner out, I thought, "This is going to be hard for him. Certainly awkward." Andy's thought was simply, "The more awkward, the better." Actually, the only awkward part was the invitation because he knew, and I knew, this wasn't his idea. From there, it was a great dinner, easy conversation, and a sincere apology. The cost was high for a sixteen-year-old guy, but the relationship was truly restored, and we both knew it. You know how defining moments stick with you? To this day, I have a snapshot in my head of where we were sitting, what we were eating, and even the shirt he was wearing. I think it was the same for him. And *that's* why it was Andy's finest parenting moment.

When your children are young, include them in decisions about how to make things up to someone they've hurt. Guide them with questions like, What do you think would make Mom feel better? What's something nice you can do for Dad? How can you show your sister you love her? Sandra would remind our kids how much I love a clean car. The point isn't to give your kids an extra task or chore. It's to help them figure out how restitution works.

This approach to discipline reinforces the idea that every act of disobedience dishonors someone. Typical methods of punishment don't reinforce much of anything relationally. Discipline connects the dots between actions and the people affected. And it teaches your child more than a lesson. It teaches them a life skill.

Before I close this chapter, two more quick discipline observations.

First observation: *Later is longer.* The day will come when you are no longer responsible for disciplining your children. Believe it or not, the day will come when you are no longer responsible for your children at all. They will be grown and gone. And not only is the grown-and-gone season later, odds are, it will also last longer. Longer than the seemingly endless season of diapers, babysitters, homework, scary friends, and social media discussions.

My point is that the nature of your "later and longer" adult relationships with your children will depend a great deal on whether you disciplined with the relationship in mind. Think about it. If you discipline with behavior modification in mind, you may in fact raise kids who behave around you and then choose not to be around you when they are old enough to choose. Nobody looks forward to dinner with the hall monitor, not to mention the fashion, grades, and hairstyle monitor. Remember, later is longer, so discipline with later in mind.

As we've already pointed out, this isn't the most *efficient* way of administering discipline. Taking stuff away is more efficient. But it's not all that effective. But efficiency and creativity are not the only barriers to this approach. Perhaps the biggest challenge of disciplining with later in mind is that if you discipline them to love you later, they may hate you now. And most parents aren't comfortable with that. Actually, none of us are *comfortable* with that. But it's certainly a potential reality during the middle school and high school years. And it's in those tense nose-to-nose moments that we are most tempted to blink, throw up our hands, and give in.

Even if you aren't overly inclined to want your child's approval, it's hard to endure their outright *dis*approval. But sometimes that's what love requires. Occasionally you have to go to bed knowing things are not well with everybody's soul. Disciplining with the relationship in mind can be tough on relationships. But the same is true for the payback punishment approach. So in case no one has told you before, it's okay if your children don't like you now if it means they will appreciate you later. Because later is longer.

Last thing: Disciplining with the *relationship* in mind is not the same as disciplining with your *reputation* in mind. In fact, disciplining with reconciliation and restoration in mind will eventually conflict with protecting your reputation. Let's face it—nobody has more potential to embarrass us than our children. And when they do, it isn't an emotionally neutral experience, is it? In those moments, our desire to discipline appropriately runs counter to our desire to protect and maintain our reputation—our reputation as a parent, an employee, a good Christian, a good person in general. To put it another way, your children's behavior and your ego are not mutually exclusive. Your pride desperately wants your children to perform well in public. That's not an accusation. It's an observation. We all want our kids to behave in a way that makes us look like all-star parents. When that doesn't happen—particularly in front of the boss or the neighbors—part of our reaction is driven by our bruised ego rather than a parenting model. When your child has a meltdown in front of the in-laws, who are already a bit suspicious about how you are raising *their grandchildren*, you'll be tempted to put your reputation ahead of your goal of relationship restoration.

But that natural conflict of interest provides you with an opportunity you do not want to miss. When your child's behavior puts your reputation on the line, it does something else as well. It provides you with a premier opportunity to demonstrate to your child that they are more important to you than your reputation in the community. Or at church. Or with the in-laws. And that is an opportunity you dare not miss, especially in the middle school and high school years. By then your kids are intuitive enough to discern when discipline is born out of your concern for them versus your concern for your own reputation. Disciplining with the relationship in mind is more important than ever when your kids know your reputation took a hit because of their behavior.

When I was in eighth grade, about forty-nine years ago . . . let that sink in for a moment . . . I had a conversation with my dad that I remember to this day. I didn't realize it at the time, but it was a defining moment in terms of my understanding of where I stood in relation to his desire to protect his reputation. Our reputations are important. Our children are important. These are both values. But some values take precedence over others. Our children are watching and experiencing how we prioritize our values and how we prioritize them. One misguided response or remark has the power to undo years of affirmation.

As you may know, my dad was a pastor. When I was in elementary school, we moved to Atlanta, where he eventually became the senior pastor at the First Baptist Church of Atlanta located downtown. More specifically for this story, it was located three blocks east of the Varsity, the world's largest drive-in restaurant. Most customers at the Varsity ordered from and ate in their cars, but the restaurant did have a few eating rooms. (It would be too generous to call them dining rooms.) Each was the same, with plastic chairs connected to plastic tables all facing toward a television hanging from the ceiling in the corner.

During our middle school years, my friend Louie Giglio and I had a habit of sneaking off to the Varsity after Sunday school instead of attending the worship service. We would order food, find an empty eating room, stand up on one of the chairs, and manually change the channel on the television to channel 5, where our church service was broadcast live. Then we would pay just enough attention to my dad's sermon to be able to comment on it intelligently on the ride home with our parents. We wouldn't lie. We would deceive. Which is worse.

One Sunday after church, my dad and I were driving home in our green Grand Safari station wagon. I was sitting directly behind him, so there was no eye contact. At some point in our conversation, he said, "Evelyn [his secretary] told me that someone told her they saw you and Louie leaving the church property after Sunday school and it looked like you might be headed to the Varsity." Then he paused. I didn't say anything. I assumed what was coming next. And I assumed it wouldn't be pleasant. First Baptist Church of Atlanta was the largest church in the city of Atlanta. My dad was a public figure. He had a reputation to protect. And it certainly reflected poorly on him that his son was skipping church to eat chili dogs at the drive-in down the street. And as Evelyn made clear, people were talking.

After what seemed like an eternity, he said something I

would never forget. But when he said it, he had no idea I would never forget it. He said, "And do you know what I told her?"

"No, sir," I said.

He said, "I told her to tell her friend to raise her own children and I'll raise mine."

Silence.

That was it.

There was no "But if I hear about you and Louie . . ." He dropped it. Never brought it up again. And I felt drawn in rather than pushed away. I felt important. I felt like my dad sided with me rather than against me. I didn't have words for it then. But at a level I probably couldn't discern as an eighth grader, I knew I was more important to my dad than his public reputation. His ego was in check. He put me first. And I felt it. I still feel it. That was some good parenting. That was good disciplining. That was disciplining with the *end* in mind. With the *relationship* in mind. And I never forgot it. And Louie and I were in the second row the following Sunday.

In a way, that was a defining moment for me. And, this is important, a *defining* moment is better than a *teachable* moment. Defining moments are easy to miss when our ego is not in check, when our reputation is on the line. So discipline with the relationship in mind. If you do, in time your reputation as a parent will be restored. Because later is longer.

CHAPTER 6

Schedule Survival

(SANDRA)

Fall 1995 was a terrible time to start a church. Not globally, but personally.

Andy and five former staff members of his dad's church decided to launch North Point Community Church (if you're curious about that story, see chapter 2 of *Deep & Wide*) at the exact time he and I had two toddlers waddling around in diapers and a baby due any day.

Maybe you know, maybe you don't: starting a church is a lot. Andy worked in the office all day, had dinners and meetings scheduled some evenings, and preached on the weekends.

Meanwhile, I was at home with two preschoolers, getting ready for a newborn. Maybe you know, maybe you don't: that season of parenthood is also a lot. We were short on margin, especially in our schedule.

We weren't naive about how demanding it would be to

build a church and grow a family simultaneously. We anticipated the obligations that would pull Andy away from home and the responsibilities I would have to handle solo as a result. We were both willing to play our parts to get it all done. The question was, Were there enough hours in the day?

The answer: *No.*

We quickly discovered that if Andy stayed at work until every last task was accomplished, he'd never make it home. If he stayed at home until the kids got all the attention they craved, he'd never make it to work. And even for a task-oriented person like me, getting through everything on our family's to-do list was not even close to possible. Trust me. I tried.

Tensions grew as the months wore on, both of us grinding through exhausting hours. We hit a wall and realized the unsustainability of our situation. That led to one of the most crucial conversations and one of the most important decisions of our marriage.

If we were going to survive this season, we needed an overhaul of the Stanley family schedule.

The dilemma we faced back then is not unique to us. You've likely experienced your own version. The demands of work, both inside and outside the home, and the demands of parenting are destined to be at odds.

So I *should* kick off our discussion of family scheduling addressing that tension, but I'm not going to. Andy has already tackled that topic in his book *When Work and Family Collide.* (I know I'm not an unbiased reviewer, but I think every working parent should read it.) I'll leave it to him to make the case for putting your family before your career, but I do want to share one anecdote from the book.

One day Andy was talking with a busy corporate VP about juggling work and home. This man mentioned over and over how much he loved his wife and kids, until eventually Andy interrupted and said, "You love your family in your heart, but they can't see your heart. You have to love them on your calendar."

Ouch.

Point made.

But I'll restate it anyway. How we spend our time telegraphs a message to our loved ones. We can *say* we love our families, every hour on the hour. But what we spend our time on is what really communicates. It communicates either acceptance or, regrettably, rejection to the people closest to us.

Especially to our kids.

Sure, the busy executive loved his children. But how were they supposed to know that? What conclusion could they draw except that Dad's work was more valuable and more interesting than they were?

To kids, time is the currency of love.

This is great news. Stick with me for a second. Your calendar is a powerful, practical way to communicate love to your kids. And who primarily controls your calendar? If you're honest, *you do*.

Your presence—on the sidelines or at the dinner table—sends your kids the message that they matter, that they are worthy, that they are valuable and even interesting to you.

Yes, you love them in your heart. But for them to grow up knowing it, for them to feel it, you have to love them on your calendar.

Now let's get a bit more practical.

We had established our primary parenting objective already, our *it*. Achieving that parenting objective relied on everyone reaching adulthood with our relationships intact. Because of that, we had a litmus test for decisions about our schedule:

Is this good for our relationships?

If the answer was yes, we would do it. Here's what that looked like.

- Are piano lessons for the kids good for our relationships? Yes. Music is important to Andy, and he's excited to share that passion with them.
- Is a planned weekend getaway without the kids good for our relationships? Yes. Making our marriage a priority

and modeling that for our kids brings stability and security to us and to them.

- Is using my time to launch a new ministry at church good for our relationships? No. It will stretch me too thin to be the kind of mom and wife I want to be. Participating in ministry, yes. Carrying the responsibility of launching a new initiative while having toddlers at home, no.
- Are Andy's travel and speaking opportunities good for our relationships right now? No. This season is busy enough, and the demands of building a church are all-consuming.

Applying this question to our schedule made it obvious what should stay, what should go, what should increase, and what should be dialed back. Asking it day after day was how we brought clarity to the chaos of our family calendar. Asking it year after year was how we continued moving toward our goal as our kids grew up.

The answers Andy and I landed on changed categorically as our family moved through the different parenting stages. I called them my "categorical nos."

Pre-Kids

Before Andrew was born, Andy and I had the freedom to say yes to almost everything. We worked together and traveled together a lot. Just about the only things we scratched from our schedule were ones that would stretch us too far financially. They failed the litmus test of being good for our relationship.

Little Kids

Once we were entrenched in life with little kids, we said no to almost everything. We categorically declined invitations that would rob us of time at home. Andy passed up opportunities that required him to travel. We both paused our most time-consuming hobbies, especially Andy. I'll let him explain.

I have a good bit of musical ability and a lot of musical interest. I played in bands throughout high school and college. I've written a couple dozen songs. I even wrote a musical. Like most musicians, I had accumulated quite a collection of gear through the years: recording equipment, guitars, keyboards, drum machines, and several miles of cable. It was an expensive and time-consuming hobby. When Sandra and I married, she encouraged me to pursue my passion. I built out a small studio in the basement of our condominium. The challenge was that once I entered my little studio, time stood still. For me, anyway. It was not unusual to retreat to my studio after dinner and emerge just in time for breakfast. Four years after we were married, Andrew was born. Twenty months later, Garrett was born. As Andrew looked less like a baby and more like a little boy and, consequently, needed and deserved more of my time, I realized something had to give. Actually, something had to go. A few months before Garrett was born, I made a decision. Surprisingly, it was one of the easiest decisions I've ever made. But it came as a shock to those who knew my love for music. I decided to sell my studio gear. Not just pack it away for another day. Sell it.

Why? I could see a storm brewing on the horizon. I knew I would be torn between my family and the studio. And my vision for my family dictated that I put my musical pursuits on hold. There was no way I could develop the relationship I envisioned with my children while pursuing my musical aspirations.

Vision has a way of prioritizing or reprioritizing our values.

Sandra and I had a clear vision of what we wanted for our family. I had a clear vision for the kind of relationship I wanted with my children. Music mattered, but it didn't matter most. So during that season of my life, I set it aside. It was one of several no-for-now-but-not-forever decisions. It's one I have never regretted.

Older Kids

I homeschooled our kids through most of their elementary years. It was a task that demanded my undivided attention, so I didn't add much else to my schedule. I didn't try to juggle a side hustle. I didn't make plans to meet regularly with friends for coffee or lunch. I didn't mentor young moms or take charge of any areas of ministry at church. It was best for our family that I stayed as focused as possible.

Once the homeschooling season had passed, I felt freer to thoughtfully add things back to my personal calendar. More flexibility in our schedule allowed us to become a foster family. The rhythm was different, but there was margin for a few more yeses.

Empty Nest

Now that we've reached the season of life without kids living under our roof, we say yes to things that have been categorical nos for years. We can travel for work and fun. Andy puts in longer hours at the office and has more space for creative pursuits. I headed back to school for a graduate degree and ventured into some writing projects. The discipline of saying no during other seasons got us to our goal of adult children who like being around us and each other. And now we have plenty of time to spend with them.

That's not to say declining opportunities was easy.

Being in ministry with Andy often brought unique opportunities my way. Opportunities with amazing impact potential. Opportunities for leading people to faith in Christ. Opportunities to build personal influence and be a major contributor to women's events and broader ministry environments. It also presented a platform of influence that I felt a real responsibility to steward well.

Sometimes great speaking or leading opportunities got plopped in my lap, some involving travel to cool places. And when you're wiping noses and bottoms all day, every day and an invitation to jet off somewhere fun and be treated like you're important comes along? Well, that is no small temptation.

Even harder, occasionally I had opportunities to leverage my influence for the good of some kids in hard places or a movement that tugged at my heartstrings. Sadly, I usually knew I had to say no.

During those difficult-decision years and heavy wiping-stuff years, my mom was my go-to for encouragement. A daily dose of her wisdom was a lifeline for me as a young mom. No matter my frustration, her counsel was always the same: *This is only a season.*

That piece of wisdom became foundational to my parenting. It was a reminder to savor each stage. It was an encouragement to be patient. Before I knew it, our kids would outgrow whatever was bothering me that day. Most of all, though, it was an incredible comfort when I had to say no to something I wanted to do.

I was saying no for now, not forever.

The time would come when I'd be able to say yes more frequently. Opportunities would still be there—sometimes even better ones.

The same is true for you. When you have to say no for now, maybe my mom's wisdom will help you as much as it helped me. You are not saying no forever. *This is only a season.*

I promise you this: giving up something *now* for something better *later* is not a sacrifice, it's an investment.

And standing where I now stand, with kids in their twenties, I can tell you one more thing with confidence: the return on that investment is 100 percent worth what you give up on the front end. Trust me on that.

I also experienced an unexpected by-product of my no-for-now posture. As difficult as it sometimes was to say no to someone who graciously offered an opportunity to me, a weird phenomenon kept happening. I say "kept happening" . . . it happened at least a handful of times.

My response was typically something along the lines of, "Wow. Thank you for thinking of me. That sounds like something I'd love to say yes to. But I've decided that in this season, with the ages of my kids, I need to keep my focus in place. I need to say no for now."

Sometimes I would get a blank stare. Like, "What are these weird words you are saying right now?" And then, sometime later, that person would circle back with something along the lines of, "Sandra, when you told me you were saying no because you were trying to stay focused in that season of parenting your kids, I realized for the first time that saying no was, in fact, an option. Thanks for letting me see that it's okay to do that."

It was like they just needed to hear someone else say no, giving them permission to say it too. Who knew?

Beyond looking at your family's schedule and asking, "Is this good for our relationships?" there is one more factor to consider as you decide how to spend your time. It's a complicated sentence but a simple idea.

There is cumulative value to little deposits of time made consistently over a long period of time.

In other words, little deposits of time over a long period of time have a big payoff in the end. It's like saving money consistently. It's like regularly saying no to the donuts in the break room. It's like chipping away, slowly but surely, at debt.

The most obvious example is exercise. We all know that exercising thirty minutes day after day, month after month, year after year has significant results. The same is true for practicing a foreign language or musical instrument, studying for an exam, or spending time with your kids.

Consistently investing small amounts of time over a long period of time will have an extraordinary payoff for your relationships.

This concept was huge for us.

We made a nightly habit of sitting down for family dinner around our table at home. Andy and I committed that small bit of time to our family every day for nearly two decades.

The value of this practice was not in any one dinner. Pick an evening at random from the years we had multiple high chairs and booster seats pulled up to the table and you might say it didn't appear valuable at all—except to Shadow, our black Lab, who counted on slippery toddler hands or inexperienced cutlery use to guarantee his next treat.

That's because there is no immediate benefit to a single installment of time. Our kids weren't more connected the morning after any particular meal. The value accrues slowly over time—so slowly that it's easy to mistakenly think there *is* no value.

Skip a single installment and there's no consequence either. For long-game habits like family dinner, you don't pay an immediate price for opting out one time. Stay late at the office or agree to a dinner meeting and nothing much happens. In the absence of any real consequence, it's easy to question the worth of the whole idea. But just as the value of investing time in your family accumulates over time, so does the cost of neglect.

We probably all know someone whose parent didn't see the cost of their choices adding up. The dad who kept meaning to leave the office in time for the Little League games. The season ended and he had missed his son's big and small successes. The parent who underestimated the accumulated health impact of perpetual "one more night" of drive-through dinners and eating in the van. Eventually everyone's health took a hit.

They never got around to making small investments of time, over time, and they missed the big payoff. I want your family to experience the payoff. It is worth the effort.

What can you tweak in your daily schedule right now so your investment of time has a cumulative effect? I enjoy cooking, so eating dinner together was an obvious choice for something we'd do consistently as a family. What we ate wasn't what mattered, it was the habit of gathering at home around the table.

As the kids got older and busier, it got trickier. At the beginning of the week, I'd look at our various schedules and find the nights that would work. I'd fire off a family text: "Dinner at home Monday, Tuesday, and Thursday." Even after the kids moved out, I'd occasionally text a schedule of the nights they were welcome to come home and join Andy and me.

Obviously, gathering for dinner is not a perfect fit for every family. It doesn't have to be. The principle behind it is the important thing: *There is cumulative value to little deposits of time made consistently over a long period of time.* Arrange your schedule accordingly and I guarantee you won't regret it.

Let's return to the conversation and decision that changed our family's course, though we hardly knew it at the time. Andy was running himself ragged launching the church, and I was wearing myself out at home.

At our breaking point, Andy looked at me and asked, "What would *ideal* look like?" In terms of his schedule, he wanted to know what I was wishing for. If I could press a magic button and have his schedule conform to my ideal, what would that look like?

Any parent with young kids knows firsthand the pinch of the late afternoon. Or maybe *chaos* is a better word. It's that point when your patience is short, your task list is long, and the kids are getting cranky. Some people call it the "witching hour." I don't know what that means exactly, but it seems to fit.

Every afternoon, I was grinding through dinner prep with toddlers underfoot, and by the time Andy walked through the door, I was *done*. If I'm honest, I was kind of mad. But he hadn't done anything wrong. He was trying to do ministry and provide for his family. Such a terrible guy, right?

So my answer to Andy's question? "In a perfect world, I would love for you to be home by four every afternoon."

Even as I heard myself say it, I knew it was an unreasonable request. Full-time employees (much less founders) don't clock out at 4:00 p.m. But he had asked what would be ideal, and that was it.

At their next staff meeting—*staff* being a generous term since there were only six of them—Andy told the team he was adjusting his schedule. He could meet anyone as early as they wished in the morning, but he was heading home at 4:00 p.m.

I remember several occasions when someone asked for a 5:00 or 6:00 meeting (thinking p.m., not a.m.), and Andy's response was, "Sure, what breakfast places are open that early?" Gosh, I love him.

In the years since he made that decision, Andy has talked about the fears that came along with it. Would his team think he was lazy? Would the people who were financially supporting the church question his commitment? What would be left undone at work while he was at home with us?

Those fears whispered loudly, but as he recalls, one insight made them possible to overcome: His roles at home were unique to him. His role at work was not.

He was the only person who could be my husband, my parenting partner, and our kids' dad. If he left a gap at home, no one else could fill it. I wasn't married to or parenting with anyone else. The kids had only one dad. He was uniquely gifted for his work at church, but it *could* be done by someone else.

Moreover, work could wait. Meetings could be postponed. Phone calls could be made another day. But kids insist on growing up now. The stages are quick, and you can't go back. There's only one first baseball season, first loose tooth, last dance recital. If you miss milestones at home, you don't get a redo.

Don't give up what's unique to you for something someone else can do.

That became a resounding statement that rattled around in our thoughts and family conversations. Still does, actually.

Decades down the road from the decision to schedule around family first, it's easy to see what we gained. We would make the same decision again every single time. It put our priorities in order, strengthened our marriage, and gave us great memories with the kids.

But I have to acknowledge that at the time, in the mundane moments, it was hard to know what hung in the balance.

Scheduling around family felt more like simple time management, like a calendar hack or efficiency gain was all we needed.

In real time, it's hard to zoom out enough to see your family's schedule as more than a logistic to manage. It may be tough for you to imagine the potential impact of your decision to train for a marathon right now or to sign your child up for yet another activity.

Your time is too valuable and your family too precious to let the current of culture carry you. It may drop your family at a destination you weren't aiming for—experience rich but relationship poor. It's a terrible, and costly, trade. Use your schedule to protect and enrich your relationships instead.

Making the tweaks, the changes, the overhauls pays off. Your *it* will be within reach. And on the other side, in all likelihood you'll end up with kids who want to be with you and with each other even when they no longer have to be.

CHAPTER 7

Words

(ANDY)

Somewhere along the way, you were told, "Actions speak louder than words." When it comes to sizing up a person's character, that's probably true. When it comes to parenting, I'm not so sure.

I'm not convinced actions are *louder*.

They're certainly loud.

But within the context of the parent-child relationship, words are abnormally loud. While most words carry *some* weight, parent-to-child words carry extraordinary weight. Words play such a dominant role in the parent-child relationship that what's *not* said often impacts children more than what *is* said. I've never had anyone of any age quote to me what a friend, neighbor, spouse, or coworker *never* said to them. But dozens, perhaps hundreds, of students, singles, married adults, and senior adults have quoted, with tears in their eyes, a three- or four-word sentence their father *never* said:

"I love you."

"I'm proud of you."

If either or both of those sentences caused you to get a bit misty or put a lump in your throat, you get it. But let's not rush by it. It's important to realize we can influence the trajectory of our children's lives through words *not spoken*.

I'm not sure it's possible to overstate the impact of a parent's words, both expressed and unexpressed. While I doubt many parents would disagree with that assessment, Sandra and I have seen too many parents either refuse to or forget to *pivot* when it comes to the tone and words they choose when communicating with their children. It's easy to forget the *weight* of our words.

Influence Is Everything

The goal of successfully negotiating the minefield of words is not so our children will grow up thinking we are nicer than we actually are. The goal of proper word and tone choices goes beyond building and protecting their self-esteem. The reason we must get this right is far more self-serving than any of those things. The reason is *influence*.

Parents with adult children will be quick to tell you to

preserve the influence! Never give up influence with your kids unnecessarily. By the time they're ten, that's pretty much all you've got. Because once your kids hit double digits, you can't *make* them do anything.

Yes, you read that correctly.

You can bribe and threaten. But in the end, if your son chooses not to get out of bed, make his bed, or get on the bus, you're out of luck. You can *keep* your children from doing things. You can *discipline* your kids for *not* doing things. But you can't *make* them do anything. I remember when Garrett and I first collided with this uncomfortable reality.

When Garrett was somewhere around ten, every time I asked him to do something he wasn't in the mood to do—which, as for so many kids, was most things—he developed the annoying habit of responding with, "Do I have to, Dad?"

For a long time I responded with, "Yes, Garrett, you have to." To which he would respond, "Yes, sir," and then he would go about whatever it was I had asked him to do.

"Garrett, I need you to take the trash can down to the street."

"Do I have to, Dad?"

"Yes, Garrett, you have to."

"Yes, sir, Dad."

This went on for so long that I began adding, "And yes, you have to," before he had time to ask.

"Garrett, I need you to take the trash can down to the street. And yes, you have to."

Then one day it dawned on me: he *doesn't* have to. I can't

make Garrett do anything. So the next time he asked if he had to, I surprised him with, "Actually, you don't have to."

That got his attention. But it led to a follow-up question. "What happens if I don't?"

Before I tell you what I said next, a quick disclaimer: I don't know if this was good parenting. I do know it made a dent. So take it with a grain of salt. I said, "Garrett, now that you're ten years old, you don't have to do anything I ask you to do."

"I don't?"

"Nope. You don't have to because I can't *make* you. In fact, from this moment on, no one can make you do anything. They can *keep* you from doing things or punish you for not doing things. But no one can make you do anything."

Then I paused for effect.

"Garrett, this is why we have prisons. Prisons are for people who wouldn't do what they were supposed to do. And now they can't do what they want to do."

His annoying habit didn't end immediately. But mine did. From then on, when he would ask if he had to, I responded, "No, you don't have to." Because he didn't. But he did anyway.

I think the prison thing had an effect.

All that to say, once your children hit double digits, you're down to influence, bribes, and threats. And if your *it* includes a healthy adult relationship with your kids, the sooner you dispense with bribes and threats the better. Building and preserving influence is the way forward. And *influence* is directly related to *respect*. We are open to the influence of people we respect. We naturally resist the influence of those for whom we have little or no respect, even when we suspect they might be right.

I know a young man whose father made a lot of money in the financial services industry, but the son refuses to listen to, much less act on, his father's financial advice. He lost respect for his father years ago and can't get past it.

If influence is a tool, respect is like a tool belt. Lose the belt, lose the tool. To take this weak analogy a step further, the buckle on the belt is made up of *say* and *do*. Two things govern a child's respect for their parents: what they *say* and what they *do*. So what we say and how we say it is a big deal. Our words are connected to our influence. Never give up influence unnecessarily. Choose your words wisely.

A Word about Words

Every time you speak to your children, three dynamics determine how they process what they hear.

1. Words are not equally weighted.
2. Source determines weight.
3. Intent is irrelevant.

These dynamics are at work whether you know them or not and whether you leverage them or not. Taking these into consideration when talking with your kids will all but ensure they hear what you *say*, not what you accidentally *communicate*.

Big difference.

Not only are all three dynamics at play in every conversation, but all three are also at play in every season of parenting. Nobody outgrows these. We've all been on the receiving end of all three, which makes it even more bewildering that we so easily lose sight of these dynamics when it comes to our own children. To begin with,

Words are not equally weighted.

Depending on which study you read, it takes anywhere between five and nine positive comments to counterbalance one negative comment. But those stats pertain to marriage and marketplace relationships. How many affirming parental comments are required to counterbalance a parent's less-than-affirming or critical comment?

I don't know. But I would bet more than nine.

Negative words always weigh more than positive words. This is true for every relationship. It's especially true in the parent-child relationship. You probably don't remember much of anything you said to your parents when you were young. But there are things they said to you that you'll never forget.

All that good advice? In one ear, out the other. The conversations that began with "Son, never forget . . . ," we forgot. But the negatives? The critical, cynical, comparison comments? Those arrows were barbed. They stuck. They held fast. And they hurt.

When I was sixteen my goal was to look as much like

Peter Frampton as possible. Your parents may remember Peter. I had the hair to pull it off. But pulling it off meant not cutting it off. My mom thought my thick, curly head of hair was beautiful. My dad thought it made me look like a girl.

And he told me so.

He wasn't wrong. My kids look at my high school pics and stare in disbelief.

I can still remember walking into the kitchen after consenting to get my hair cut shortish. Dad looked up from his chair and said, "Now you look like my son." I still remember what I thought in that moment: "Whose son did I look like an hour ago?"

While I aspired to look like Peter, I wanted to play and sing like Elton. But I never took piano lessons because, well, girls took piano lessons. I did take guitar lessons and quickly discovered chords on the piano. So I banged out octaves with my left hand and chords with my right, which meant every song sounded pretty much the same. I know that to be the case because my dad told me that as well.

How did I respond to those father wounds? That criticism?

I followed in his footsteps and worked for him for ten years. Because those weren't the only things he said to me.

My point in breaking your heart with those two excerpts from my rock-and-roll years is that negative words cut deep. They have staying power. Branding power. Odds are, we'll all slip up from time to time and wound the folks we love most. There's probably no way to avoid that other than to die early. This is why it's imperative that we counterbalance the accidental and occasional killer words with intentional life-giving words. Negatives must be the exception rather than the rule. And my dad was great at that.

He called me "son number one." He gave me a jersey with a number one on the front and back. Granted, I was his only son. But the way he said it made me feel like I was number one of many. There was never a season he didn't tell me how proud he was of me. He came to every baseball game. He watched me ride the bench through several basketball seasons. His exceptions were exceptions. So we survived.

In my mother's eyes, I could do no wrong. She loved to hear me bang the piano out of tune. And then she would pay to have it retuned. Actually, she would pay to have it repaired. Did you know you can break the strings on a piano by banging the keys too hard?

I did not know that until I did it.

But even with all her over-the-top affirmation, the conversation I remember most clearly was not positive. I had just wrapped up my second semester of college. After my first semester I made the list: the academic warning list. At the end of my second semester, I made a second list: academic probation.

Strike two.

Upon receiving that short but disturbing letter from Georgia State University, my mom said she wanted to talk to me about school. I, of course, expected the traditional, "You can do this, son! You can do anything you set your mind to! Climb every mountain. Ford every stream. Follow every rainbow!"

Instead, she sat me down at the kitchen table, reached across, took my hand, looked me in the eye, and said, and I quote, "Andy, college isn't for everyone."

"Everyone?"

I was the only other person in the house. She was talking about me! College wasn't for me! My own mom didn't think I had what it took to finish college. And her saying that was exactly what it took to get me to finish college.

Negative words are essential at times. Parents who can't bring themselves to deliver the bad news aren't much better off than parents who are all bad news. But remember, words aren't equally weighted. The negatives weigh more than the positives. Our children need a lot of positives because those positives equip them to endure, properly assimilate, and learn from the negatives. It's not enough to tell your children what they need to hear. You have to prepare them to hear it.

If you don't prepare the soil, the seed won't take root.

Some of the most *important* things you say to your children are also some of the most *negative*. Correction is essential. So it's essential your children are able to digest and apply your words of correction. That probably won't happen unless negative words are the exception rather than the rule.

To the dads: If you're a man of few words but the negative words come easy, you may have some work to do. If you want your correction to impact your kid's direction, you may need to adjust your positive to negative ratio. You're probably familiar with the phrase *portion control*. This is *proportion control*. If you don't adjust your proportion of positives to negatives, your correcting will undermine your connecting, and eventually you will lose influence. It's possible to be *right* and *right* your kid *right* out the door. We've seen it. Perhaps you have as well. So don't do that. Don't be content with being right. If all you do is correct, you may always be correct. But relationships don't thrive on correction. Relationships thrive on connection.

The Bad Guy

In two-parent homes the role of disciplinarian generally falls to one parent over the other. If that's you, a word of caution: Because of the weighted-words dynamic, you may find that your role as disciplinarian begins to define your relationship with your kids. That's no fun for anybody. I know because I played that role in our home, and early on I did a poor job with my positive to negative words ratio.

This became painfully obvious every time I mentioned to one of my kids that I needed to ask them something or talk to them about something. Their immediate response was, "Am I in trouble?"

I remember asking my dad the same question when he mentioned needing to chat with me. Honestly, I'm *still* tempted to ask him that when he calls and says he needs to chat with me. So to some degree it goes with the territory. But there are things we can do to avoid being relegated to the assistant principal role at home.

The solution isn't to avoid disciplining our children so they will like us more. If you do that, they may like you more now but will respect you less later. Later is longer. Besides, less respect leads to less influence. So don't abdicate your role. Instead, double down on the positives. It's all about the ratio. Positive words maintain the connection necessary for effective correction.

Again, our words aren't equally weighted. Negatives, even constructive negatives, weigh more than positives. Negatives are necessary. But for the necessary negatives to have a positive effect, they must be, once again, the exception rather than the rule. When that's not the case, negatives become noise. After a while our kids aren't listening. They aren't learning. They're just biding their time.

We've been told it's possible to have too much of a good thing. That may be true in some arenas of life, although nothing comes to mind at the moment. But it is certainly not the case when it comes to affirming words spoken to a child by their parents. No one traces their adult problems back to parents who were too proud or too encouraging. This is the one area of life where you can't overdo it.

But go ahead and try.

Somebody will be glad you did.

Consider the Source

So the first dynamic that determines what your children *hear* regardless of what you actually *say* is that *words are not equally weighted*. The second follows from the first:

Source determines weight.

The weight of words is determined by the source of those words. Ladies, if your best girlfriend comments on how cute your outfit is and how young it makes you look, those words weigh five pounds. But if your fifteen-year-old daughter walks by the kitchen, pauses, and says the same thing the same way with the same enthusiasm?

I know.

Only in your dreams.

But for illustration's sake, imagine if such a thing actually happened. Words that weighed a mere five pounds at the coffee shop weigh forty-five pounds in the kitchen.

Not because of the *environment*.

Because of the *source*.

Source determines weight.

When my administrative assistant, Diane Grant, knows I'm headed to someone's office to deliver not so good news or a not so positive evaluation, she frequently and appropriately reminds me, "Remember, your words weigh a thousand pounds."

Why *remember*?

Because it's so easy to forget.

On other occasions she'll say, "I think you should let me handle this conversation. My words don't weigh as much." Diane recognizes what's easy to miss in both corporate and family contexts. When it comes to words,

> Source determines weight.
> Weight determines impact.
> Impact determines outcome.

If physics is your thing . . . I know. Humor me.

Parent Words

It took a minute for me to recognize how this dynamic was playing out in our home.

I can't count the times I had to go back upstairs to apologize, not for what I *intended* to communicate but for what I *unintentionally* communicated because I was the one communicating it. I had to learn to take *me* into account. And Sandra would tell you that as the kids got older, she had to learn to take herself into account as well. Some words were best delivered by me. Some were best delivered by her. And then, just when we had it all figured out—puberty. The deck got reshuffled.

There comes a time in a young man's life when it's difficult to hear what his mother is saying *because* his mother is saying it.

Just saying.

One size fits all may work for hospital gowns, but not so much when it comes to communicating with our kids. Words matter. And the source of those words matters. The right words delivered by the wrong person can cause things to go terribly wrong. When you find yourself sitting at the kitchen table, staring at your spouse, mumbling, "All I said was . . . ," you may have chosen the wrong words, or you may have been the wrong person to deliver those words.

When you walk into your son's or daughter's bedroom to

deliver some not so good news, you see a child who knows better, was taught better, and has the potential to do better.

But who do they see?

They see the person whose approval they want more than anything else in the world.

When choosing your words, don't forget to take *you* into account.

Unfair Advantage

Sandra and I are foster parents. We've had a dozen or so kids in and out of our home through the years. Interacting with the birth parents of children in foster care isn't always encouraged or even possible. But occasionally it works out. In two instances, we were able to contact—and in one instance stay in contact with—parents working toward reunification with their children.

I'll never forget a phone conversation with a single mom who had recently been allowed to bring her two young children back into her home. The purpose of my call was to congratulate and encourage her. I commended her for completing her counseling. I told her I was proud of her for getting back on her feet financially and for choosing to finish school. I commented on how lucky her children were to have her as their mom. I poured it on. And I meant every word of it. When I finally ran out of superlatives—silence.

Nothing.

I was about to ask if she was still there when I heard her whisper, "I wish my dad would say that."

Encouragement was nice coming from me. But my five-pound words only served to remind her of the fifty-pound words only a daddy can deliver.

Same words.

Different source.

Significantly different impact.

What she didn't say is as instructive as what she did. She didn't say, "I wish my dad *thought* that," or "I wish my dad *felt* that way."

She longed to hear him *say* it.

I'd gotten to know her dad. He was not a good dad. But he was *her* dad. His words weighed more than mine. A lot more.

Which brings me to a disturbingly inequitable but mostly true reality. After forty years of ministry experience, I'm convinced that if a mother's words weigh fifty pounds, a father's words weigh, well, usually they weigh more. And no, that's not fair. It should be the other way around. Our mothers' words should weigh more because they risked more to get us safely into this world. They put their lives on the line while we dads watched from the sidelines or watched daytime television in the waiting room. So no, it's not fair. But it's often true. A father's words weigh more. There's something about the acceptance and approval of a father that runs extra deep. And there's something about the rejection and disapproval of a father that cuts extra deep.

Some Things Never Change

If you ask Sandra to describe the moment she felt most affirmed as a mom, she won't recount an incident involving one of our children. She'll tear up and tell you about a short exchange she had with her dad.

She was perched on a stool in the kitchen feeding Andrew, who had just turned one. Her dad came downstairs, paused to watch for a moment, and said, "You are a really good mom."

Time stood still.

For her.

Not for you. Not for me. Surely there are more epic, interesting, and affirming mother moments than that. She was feeding a baby! Even bad mothers feed their babies.

But that's the point.

It wasn't memorable because of *what* she was doing. It was because of *who* recognized and commented on what she was doing. Sandra taught all three kids to read, write, and multiply. She threw elaborate birthday parties. She bungee jumped with Andrew. She learned to knit because Allie wanted to learn to knit. She feigned gratitude when Garrett surprised her with spinners for the wheels of her minivan as a Christmas gift. I taught our kids all the bad words. But it was Sandra who took the time to teach 'em all the possible combinations. And she took our kids to Homeschool Day at Six Flags.

Yes, that's a thing.

Andrew says that if you didn't know better, you would

assume it was Denim and Not-All-the-Way-Rubbed-In-Sunscreen Day at Six Flags.

The point being, as a mom, Sandra has a lot to be proud of. She has dozens of epic moments to reflect on and celebrate. But if we stacked 'em all up on one side of the affirmation scale and dropped those six words from her father on the other side?

Pop wins.

Source determines weight.

Sometimes a father's words weigh most of all.

The Sarcasm-Free Zone

Your positive deposits do more good than you assume. And your thoughtless, careless negative comments do more damage than you suspect. This is why you should make your home a *sarcasm-free zone*. Your words weigh too much. Dispense with humor that lands at the kid's expense. Or their friend's.

Your words weigh too much.

It doesn't matter that you were kidding. That you didn't really mean it. That you were just trying to be funny. Sarcasm is a power play. It's a power play that insecure men play. Your son will laugh along. Your daughter will pretend it didn't hurt. Of course they will. Your approval is more important to them than anything else in the world.

But deep down?

Behind the forced smile?

Dads, not only will your kids not take it the way you meant it, they *can't* take it the way you meant it. They don't have the capacity to. They don't see you the way you see them. And they don't feel your words the way you feel theirs.

From your perspective, you're tossing around five-pound words. At work or on the tennis court with a friend, those same words may weigh only five pounds. But your daughter isn't a work associate. Your son isn't a peer. You aren't buds, friends, or bros.

In the space between you and your kids, your words gain weight and velocity, which means your words *will* leave a mark. So decide right now to make your home a sarcasm-free zone.

You'll never regret it.

Nobody will miss it.

Pause!

Next time you catch yourself marching down the hall re-rehearsing the script you rehearsed all the way home from work, I suggest you pause outside that bedroom door and remember *who* you are and *what* you represent to the person on the other side.

If you're not confident you can communicate your approval of *who they are* along with your disapproval of *what they've done*, don't knock. You're not ready. Your perfect script will result in a less-than-perfect outcome. Because:

> Source determines weight.
> Weight determines impact.
> Impact determines outcome.

If you need to get something off your chest, call a friend, call your sister, call somebody. But don't call your kids to the kitchen. Don't unload. The bed of their truck lacks the capacity to carry what you've found ample room for in yours. You will overcommunicate. You'll talk, but you won't connect. You'll make your point, but it won't make much difference. You'll feel better. But they'll feel something else. Depending on their age, they may not have a word or a category for what they feel. Your takeaway: "She'll certainly think twice next time."

Her takeaway: "My mom hates me."

That's not *it*.

Your words carry weight.

Wield them wisely. Wield them well.

Recovery Time

When Andrew was seven years old, our favorite babysitter ran over his arm with her Honda Civic.

In our driveway.

Malisa was horrified when she realized what she'd done. Turns out it wasn't her fault. But still, when you run over any part of a child whose parents entrusted said child into your care, you feel horrible. She cried and cried. Apologized and apologized. She took full responsibility. We absolutely knew it was an accident.

But we still took Andrew to the ER.

Because there is no correlation between *intention* and *outcome*.

That it was an accident didn't alter the outcome. That it was an accident didn't lessen the pain or the trauma. When Andrew realized Malisa didn't do it on purpose, his arm didn't feel better or get better. Because there is no correlation between *intention* and *outcome*. And that brings us to the third dynamic playing in the background every time we communicate with our children:

Intent is irrelevant.

If you've ever accidentally broken a window, or your husband's favorite MLB bobblehead, or your mother-in-law's collector plate that her mother left her and her mother's mother left her, or if you've dinged somebody's car door with your car door, the same principle applies. There is no correlation between *intention* and *outcome*. It was an accident, but the window still has to be replaced, the bobblehead still has to be glued back together, and you still have to go online and search for *that* plate—ideally before she figures out you broke it. Taking responsibility is the right thing to do. But it doesn't fix anything.

As obvious as this is when it comes to broken bones, dinged doors, and shattered windows, it's not so obvious when it comes to hurt feelings. It should be. Because we've all had our feelings hurt. We've had our feelings hurt by people who love us and who didn't mean to hurt us. But knowing they didn't mean to didn't lessen the sting or shorten the recovery. Often the closer we are to someone, the more it stings and the longer it takes to get past it because, of all people, they should know better! They should know better because they know us. They love us.

Hurtful words hurt regardless of intent. There *is* a correlation between source and outcome. We've discussed that. But not intent. Unintentional words still leave a mark. Unintentional words still require recovery time.

Despite our having been on the receiving end of unintentional hurtful words, despite knowing firsthand that an apology doesn't instantly end the pain, when we're guilty of hurting someone with our words, we forget all of that and retreat to *intent*.

- I didn't mean it that way.
- That didn't come out right.
- I was trying to be funny.
- I didn't intend to hurt your feelings.

Do you know what those types of statements communicate? Blame.

You are *blaming* the person you hurt for taking what you said the way they took it. They were wrong for interpreting your words the way they did. It's *their fault* they got their feelings hurt. They should be more mature than that. Tougher than that. They should be able to read your mind and know what you meant.

Granted, blaming is rarely your *intent*. But intent is irrelevant.

Our children feel the weight of our words, not our intent.

And they feel *blame* and the associated *shame* when we couple an apology with intent. And they feel something else as well.

They feel the weight of our expectation.

Allow me to explain.

You've been there, so you should know. You've probably been there with your spouse. The scenario usually goes something like this:

You say something stupid.

They're hurt.

You apologize.

But they're still hurt. They're still mad. Distant. They want to keep talking about it. And how do you respond when your apology didn't work like a magic wand?

"I said I'm sorry!"

Implication: I expect you to be fine now. Why aren't you fine now? Why aren't we back to where we were before I said what I said? Why isn't everything okay? Doesn't saying I'm sorry turn back the clock?

Of course it doesn't.

And of course you already knew that. But there's something in all of us that wants to speed up the healing process when we're the one who inflicted the damage. But you can't rush healing. Put your full weight on that broken ankle too early and you will lengthen rather than shorten the recovery process.

Hurt is immediate. Recovery takes time.

Pressure lengthens rather than shortens recovery. Unfortunately, it's our nature as parents to attempt to artificially shorten the process of relational recovery with our children. But of course it is. We hate feeling isolated from our kids. And if we caused the isolation, we're even more inclined to shorten the recovery. We attempt to speed up their recovery to assuage our guilt. Our two favorite tools are:

- Forced proximity
- Forced forgiveness

We've probably all done it. We said something hurtful and followed up immediately with, "Come here, honey . . ." Our intent was good, but think about it. When someone hurts you, rejects you, pushes you away with their words, do you want to move toward them? Of course not. Don't require your children to come sit in your lap after you've wounded them. Don't insist on a hug unless they make the first move. Treat them like you would want to be treated. Apologize. And wait. Don't leave. Unless they ask you to. Let them choose when to move in your direction. A hug in those moments makes you feel better. A hug feels like closure. But those moments aren't about you. A compromise would be to sit beside your child. But wait for them to initiate physical contact.

Like initiating physical contact, asking your children to forgive you creates closure as well. But forgiveness is a gift. So don't ask for it, especially so close to the event that caused the hurt. You've just *taken* something from your child with your hurtful words. Don't turn right around and ask for something else too: forgiveness. They'll give it to you when they're ready. Forgiveness is part of healing. You can't rush healing. It requires time. And only the wounded know where they are in the process. So give them time. Give them space. And the older they are, the more time and space they will require. A compromise would be to say, "I hope you will forgive me."

Short and Sweet

When we wound our children with our words, our apologies should be immediate and short.

"I'm so sorry."

Then stop talking.
If you have to say something else, rinse and repeat:

"Daddy is so sorry, honey. I'm so sorry. I should not have said that. I'm so sorry."

Anything added will lessen the restorative power of your simple apology. In those tender moments, explanations sound like excuses. It's tempting to retreat to intent. Don't do it. It won't help. In the meantime, sit in your guilt as they sit in their hurt. In most cases your child will be just as anxious as you are to restore the relationship.

Resist the temptation to rush the process. There's no need to. Instead, model what it looks like to own a mistake rather than make an excuse. That's a life skill that will serve them well for the rest of their lives.

Putting It All Together

Every time you speak to your children, these three dynamics are running in the background. They determine what your children hear and feel regardless of what you say.

1. Words are not equally weighted.
2. Source determines weight.
3. Intent is irrelevant.

Taking these into consideration when talking to your kids will all but ensure they hear what you say, not what you accidentally communicate. Not only are all three dynamics at play in every conversation, but all three continue to be at play in every season of parenting. This is especially true in healthy parent-child relationships. A parent's words will always carry some weight. But in a healthy parent-child relationship, the parent's words continue to carry extraordinary weight throughout the relationship.

Before we move on from the words we use and the tone we choose, we need to touch briefly on one additional aspect of this important topic.

CHAPTER 8

When Seconds Count

(ANDY)

There is a time and place for no-two-minute-warning, voice-raised, shock-value communication with our children—namely, emergencies.

Yell only in case of emergency.

If you reserve yelling for when danger is involved, yelling will make an appropriate impression. When yelling is the norm, it won't. Before long it's just noise.

When our boys were old enough to use a public restroom without assistance, I insisted they go together and stay together until both had finished their business. One Saturday morning during their bathroom-buddy season of life, the three of us were at a big-box retailer when Andrew announced he needed to go. So off they both went. A few minutes later I looked up to see Andrew walking down the aisle without his little brother.

I reacted.

No diplomacy. No getting down on one knee and explaining to Andrew why we don't leave little brother in the bathroom alone. I was loud and direct. It had its desired effect.

Sometimes seconds count. These aren't teachable moments. These are emergency moments. I can still picture little Andrew running back down the aisle to rescue Garrett from, well, from nothing, actually, other than being alone in the men's room. But sending Andrew running closed the loop and made the point.

We did our best to prepare our kids for high-volume *emergency moments*, situations that might require Mommy and Daddy to raise their voices. Not because we were angry but because we needed their immediate, undivided attention. As part of our preparation, I asked the boys what they would do if they saw Allie step out in front of a car in a parking lot. Garrett said he would run out in front of the car so it would hit him instead.

Noble. But I suggested something different.

And we practiced it.

Quick tip: Never expect your children to know how to do something you never took the time to teach them. Seems obvious. But it's not. Do you know why some kids don't know how to behave in a restaurant? Their parents didn't practice at home. Practice makes, well, it doesn't actually *make* anything, but it certainly prepares us.

We practiced what to do during an emergency. I let the boys practice yelling at Allie and pulling her out of the street. Actually, our driveway. After all, a driveway can be a dangerous place. As you've already discovered, ours certainly was.

Anyway.

The boys enjoyed practicing and yelling at Allie. I'm not sure Allie enjoyed it. But I wanted all three kids to understand it's okay to raise our voices when we're trying to keep someone from getting hurt. There *are* times and places to raise our voices.

But not many times. And not many places. Here's why I say that. And I don't know how to say this strongly enough.

A raised voice communicates *danger*.
Danger creates *fear*.
Fear triggers fight, flight, or freeze.

The fight-flight-freeze response is not cognitive. It's not a conscious decision. It's our body's instinctive, environmentally triggered reaction to danger. It's a stress response. And that stress causes hormonal and even physiological changes. You can't control it. To the point of this chapter, your children can't control it either. If you have multiple children, they will not all react the same way to danger, real or perceived.

If you've ever been in a public place where someone suddenly began yelling, you may remember your reaction. You may remember how your body reacted. You were on defense. You didn't choose that reaction. It just happened. You didn't keep eating. You didn't keep reading or drinking your coffee.

Your head snapped up, your eyes shot wide open, and perhaps your heart started racing.

Andrew, our oldest, was at the Atlanta Hartsfield–Jackson Airport during an active shooter incident. Hearing him describe the multiple ways people responded was fascinating—mostly fleeing or freezing. He learned something about himself as well. And no, he did not attempt to tackle the shooter. I'm guessing he would have had he seen the shooter.

I'm sure I would have.

I'm sure you would have as well.

Okay, the only thing I'm actually sure of is that none of us know what we would do in a situation like that until we are in it. Andrew admitted that as he sprinted through the terminal, with no thought for anyone's safety but his own, he was looking for the Delta lounge, his assumption being that the shooter probably wasn't a Diamond Medallion Member.

Back at Home

At home, a raised voice communicates *danger*. It doesn't matter that we don't intend to communicate danger; that's what's communicated. It doesn't matter that our children aren't actually in danger. They will be afraid. Perceived danger creates *fear*. Fear triggers one of three responses. Every time. Everywhere. In every relationship.

Parents who habitually raise their voices are not teaching their children to fear the things they should fear. They are teaching their children to fear their parents, because a raised voice communicates danger, and danger creates fear.

So within the context of family,

> A raised voice should communicate danger, not anger. If there is no danger, don't raise your voice.

If you don't think you can talk to your children without raising your voice, don't talk to your children. They won't hear.

They will fear.

They will fight, flee, or freeze. What they won't do—can't do—is listen. And when it dawns on you that they aren't listening, you'll be tempted to ask, "Are you listening to me?" And they will nod. But they aren't listening. You've made it impossible for them to listen. They will hear you. But they won't hear what you're saying. What they'll hear is that you're angry and they are in danger.

We should train our children to fear the things and people that can harm them. Continue to raise your voice and pretty soon they will fear you. Their fear of you may very well drive them in the direction of the things and people they should fear. Sandra and I saw this play out over and over in our student ministry days. So one more time: A raised voice should communicate danger, not anger. If there is no danger, don't raise your voice.

Fear is an effective tool when applied purposefully and infrequently. But for fear to be *effective*, we must be *selective*.

It's a tool, not a strategy. Confuse the two and in the end your children will fear you.

That's not what you want. That's not *it*.

Facing Your Own Fears

It's possible that your high-volume communication style flows from your own fears. Perhaps you're afraid your children will make the same mistakes you did. When you sense even a trace of the behaviors, proclivities, or attitudes that led to the decisions you regret most, you, well, you just go there. You go there because you've been there. You don't want your children to end up there. That's understandable. To you. To me. But your children won't understand that until later, when the damage has already been done.

Don't allow your past failures to inform your tone and posture. The best way to ensure your kids make the same mistakes you did is to react as if they are already making the same mistakes you made. When we overreact, our kids don't feel safe. Overreact to what you see and before long you may not see it anymore. Not because anything has changed. But because your children have learned it's not safe to let you see it.

This unfortunate but common dynamic is another reason we're convinced the north star for parents is relational, not behavioral. Your negative personal history is unlikely to repeat itself through your kids if you parent with the relationship in mind. Your past may remain with you, but it does not have to define you or the way you parent. So don't parent with your past in mind. Parent with your kid's future in mind. Specifically, parent with a future relationship in mind. Maintain influence. Listen. Leverage your weighty words. And raise your voice only in case of emergency.

If you grew up in a home that felt like a constant state of emergency, I don't need to convince or remind you that that's not *it* either. That's toxic. Once you escaped, you probably never looked back and hoped never to return. You certainly didn't want to re-create that. Perhaps you've done the hard work to ensure your family history doesn't repeat itself.

But you might still have some work to do if you see yourself in any of the following scenarios:

- You sense you're doing unto others what your mother or father did unto you.
- Someone who loves you has suggested your history is beginning to repeat itself.
- One of your kids recently asked your spouse, "Why is Mommy mad all the time?" "Why is Daddy always angry?"
- If you're angry with me for even bringing it up in the first place.

Parents with unresolved anger that stems from past events or relationships are often emotionally disengaged from their children. But when they do engage, emotions escalate quickly. Angry moms and dads parent toward compliance. So children of angry parents modify their behavior. Quickly at first. But not to be better kids. They modify their behavior to avoid the sudden whirlwind that invades their space if they don't. Angry adults are generally angry with themselves. But they might know it. If you grew up with an angry parent, you can *see* it now.

But you *felt* it then.

You felt your parent's anger and felt like it was your fault. You were to blame. But nothing you did fixed it. No amount of behavior modification on your end changed anything on their end. Whatever you did, it was never enough. So depending on your temperament, talent, and opportunity, you either drove yourself crazy trying or gave up and shut down. Odds are, your brother or sister reacted the opposite way. And they couldn't win either.

Angry moms and dads reap a crop they swear they didn't sow. They swear their spouses or ex-spouses sowed it. They assume they are sowing fine, upstanding, disciplined, well-behaved citizens who will make Daddy proud. But they often reap angry young men, promiscuous young women, relationally challenged high achievers, and an empty dining room table.

Angry parents trade influence for compliance. Not intentionally. But remember, intent is irrelevant. When the middle school years roll around, angry parents discover they have neither influence nor compliance. The loss of influence in particular accelerates. When they experience their influence flagging, they double down. In most cases the tools they've used to that point are the only tools in their toolbox. Doubling down accelerates the pace of everything: less respect, less influence, less compliance, more anger, more fear, more distance. That's not *it*.

If you've seen it, you don't want it. If you grew up with it, you couldn't wait to escape it. But family history has a way of repeating itself if we don't do the work to ensure it doesn't. So if you sense you're doing unto others what your mother or father did unto you, maybe you still have some work to do.

Perhaps this will help.

Remember When

When you held her, or held him, for the first time, do you remember what you felt? What you thought? Go back to that moment. Picture those little fingers and those crusty red eyes. You were willing to *die* for that tiny bundle of life who couldn't do a thing for you.

Why not decide again what you decided then? Decide you'll do anything for that baby girl, that baby boy. This time around may require a death of sorts. You'll have to die to your pride. Die to always being right. You'll have to die to your excuses. Your self-protection. But losing those things is no great loss. They've never brought you life. Rather, they've separated you from the people you love most. They are best left behind.

When that funeral is over, you may need to forgive your dad or a stepdad. Maybe your mom. And then you'll need to forgive yourself. Sometimes that's the hardest person to forgive. And although we've never met, here's something I know about you:

You are worth forgiving.

Your heavenly Father thought so, anyway. So agree with God and forgive yourself. Then take your current parenting toolbox out back and throw it away. And start collecting some new tools.

It's not too late.

Here's how I know that: You're still their father. Their mother. Regardless of what happened in the past, your words still weigh more than you can imagine.

So use 'em well.

CHAPTER 9

Marriage Matters

(SANDRA)

Jackie and Bob are coming up on their sixtieth wedding anniversary. They've made it look pretty easy despite raising three kids, navigating the ups and downs of decades of entrepreneurship, enduring three brain surgeries and several knee replacements, traversing chapters of extended-family drama, and losing a grandchild to SIDS.

They're in their early eighties and rocking along pretty well. They're still best friends, they have a lot going on, and you rarely see one without the other. They're amazing.

And they're my parents.

About five years ago, my mom had a conversation with a young single mother who was doing some work for her. Ashley had been in and out of my parents' house regularly for a couple of years. This day, she came in seemingly carrying the weight of the world on her shoulders. Mom sat her down, poured her a cup of coffee, and began to gently pry the story out of her. Ashley's heart was hurting after a recent breakup.

Ashley looked up at my mom and said, "Mrs. Jackie, I never knew happily-ever-after was a real thing until I started watching you and Mr. Bob. And now that's what I want." Without knowing what she was saying exactly, she knew she had witnessed two imperfect people with imperfect lives who chose to choose each other every single day.

When I think of parenting and the impact our marriages have on our kids, I can't help but be grateful to my parents for the way they've navigated theirs.

As Andy mentioned in the intro, we don't presume to speak with any authority to single parents or blended families. So it would be easier, and maybe even safer, to leave marriage out of our book about parenting. This is especially true since we live in a time when 40 percent of US kiddos are born to unmarried moms.[1]

Like it or not, our marriages impact our kids, just as our parents' marriages impacted us. And we can't ignore the tension between what's *real* and what's *ideal*. What's real is that family structures are varied and impermanent. Because of divorce or death or dozens of other reasons, in and out of our control, not every family has married parents living with their kids under one roof and is surrounded by a caring and supportive community. Nonetheless, most of us agree this arrangement is ideal.

Most young ladies dreaming of their future family assume

they'll bring kids into the world with someone they love and who will work with them as partners to raise the kids all the way to the finish line.

It's what we all hope for, right?

Even when that's not possible for us, it's what we hope for our kids' families at least. Divorced parents want successful marriages for their kids. Single dads and single moms typically don't hope their kids will end up single parents too.

So Andy and I decided it's possible to hold space for what's *real* while still pointing toward what's *ideal*. And raising kids in the context of a healthy marriage is ideal.

Before we dive into some practical habits that help build a healthy marriage, let me shed some light on what shaped our thinking around this topic. As mentioned before, during our years in student ministry, Andy and I were exposed to hundreds of families. And we saw it all. Observation of real, live parents and their behaviors occasionally left us wide-eyed and wondering, like Ashley, if "happily ever after" was a real possibility. And this was in the church!

But in all those observations, as we had a clear context for the broader family dynamics, we concluded that the best parenting tool of all might be a healthy marriage.

We certainly witnessed the impact of it.

The parents we saw getting it right with their kids were getting it right in their marriage relationships too. It's like their marriages were the firm foundation for raising relationally healthy kids.

Think about it.

Your marriage—your relationship with your spouse—becomes part of the story your kids will tell. If you've ever found yourself sitting in a new small group, you know they often launch by people sharing their personal journeys. And for good reason. Understanding someone's background and story establishes a solid foundation for understanding *them*. It explains a lot about who they are. Often we walk away astounded that someone has overcome so much. And occasionally we want to pepper them with questions about how their parents created such a healthy space for their growing-up years.

Either way, parents' marriages are a huge part of adult kids' stories. Your kids are no different, and they'll have stories of their own to tell.

My grandfather passed away when my dad was twelve. My grandmother remarried six years later. Those facts are a huge part of my dad's story and a big part of mine.

Losing his father, while incredibly painful, resulted in some wonderful uncles getting involved in my father's life. These men helped shape my dad and influenced the kind of father he became. And my grandmother's second husband became the man I knew as my grandfather, also affecting multiple generations. Thankfully for us, those tricky transitions ultimately turned out to be positive ones.

The impact of those relationships outlived the relationships themselves. They always do. Good or bad. And that will be the case with your marriage too. You can't know exactly what hangs in the balance for your children and grandchildren, but you can know your marriage will be a significant part of their story.

More immediately, your marriage influences how your children move through the world *now*. The emotional climate in your home affects your children's current and future well-being.

My friend Jill spent a decade teaching elementary school. When she witnessed sudden behavioral changes in her kindergartners, she knew that something was likely amiss at home. Sadly, she saw it all the time. Parents were fighting or a separation had happened, and her previously compliant six-year-old student's behavior took a nosedive.

The two are tightly connected.

When it comes to parenting, your marriage matters. It matters a lot.

So what do we *do*? What are some practical ways to strengthen our most important human relationship? Again, we don't have all the answers, but we've been asking the questions and working on these practices for approximately thirty-four years of our thirty-four-year marriage. It's *that* big of a deal to us.

The following are some ideas for you to consider.

Prioritize and Invest

When we found out we were going to have our first kiddo, we read everything we could get our hands on and interviewed any parent who would be still long enough to have a conversation with us. One of the first things we learned was that we were *already a family* even before Andrew was born.

Some wise friends explained that having a baby didn't

make us a family. We were *already* a family. The arrival of Andrew simply made our family a little bigger. Not only were Andy and I a family *before* kids came along, we hoped to continue being a family long *after* our kids launched and had families of their own. So protecting our family meant protecting our marriage first.

I'll never forget one Sunday before we had kids. I was pregnant with Andrew, and Andy and I were in the car leaving church. The parking lot was packed, and people were waiting their turn to exit the lot.

At the same moment, Andy and I both happened to look over at the car next to us.

Here's what we saw: The husband was in the driver's seat, and the wife was in the back seat, proudly perched next to a strapped-in infant carrier. (There was a baby in it.) The front passenger seat was empty.

Andy looked at me and said, "Please never do that."

An odd request, right?

We talked some more about what we were seeing, and I gained some clarity.

Certainly nothing is inherently wrong with a mom sitting in the back seat with her baby. But in the context of Andy's request, it dawned on me for the first time that I'd have some fairly straightforward decisions to make on this parenthood journey. Those decisions would communicate to Andy either "You're my priority" or "You're not my priority now that a baby is here."

And it gave me a new lens.

Andy's simple statement informed a modus operandi I had

yet to fully develop. I think the absence of the new lens would have led me straight to a parenting strategy that formed around the squeakiest wheel. And little humans are super squeaky.

So even in the busiest seasons of parenting, we each determined to make the other feel like the priority. We talked. We planned. We budgeted. We did everything we could to mutually prioritize each other so that when the kids were gone, we'd still like each other!

One of the best practices was getting out of town, without kids, twice a year. It didn't have to be a fancy trip with flights and complicated itineraries. It could be simple and only two or three nights away. The location hardly mattered.

That's probably a lie. I like good locations.

It wasn't easy, though. And that's the pushback we've always gotten when we suggest it to other couples. Calendar issues, babysitter availability, and financial cost are all obstacles to overcome. Get creative. Trade off babysitting with a friend. Look for deals. And find ways to tuck away extra cash. Trust me, you'll be glad you did!

Here's an illustration that's funny but also a little sad. When our boys were nine and eleven, Andy coached their baseball team. One of our getaways was on the horizon, and we needed to let the parents know we wouldn't be there the following week. So when the game was over, Andy gathered the parents to see who could step in to help coach. One of the moms chimed in and said, "Wait. You and Sandra are going out of town without your kids? Is that even allowed? I don't think we've done a trip without kids since our first one was born!"

We assured the parents it was indeed allowed. And as the self-appointed chaplains of the team, we highly encouraged it.

The point is, getting away sans kids was a reset button for our relationship. And it paid big dividends when we came home refreshed and also missing our kids a little bit.

A second thing we did seems counterintuitive for the busiest season of life, but we don't regret one moment of it. In fact, it largely kept us sane.

We made our weekly small group a nonnegotiable.

During the parenting years, we really needed support and encouragement, and so did our friends. Having other couples navigating life, marriage, and parenting in the same direction as we were was life-giving. It was where we found "continuing ed" for our season of life. It was accountability and prayer support for those inevitable rough patches we all faced. And it was a weekly time to talk to adults, download our stuff, and laugh at the craziness of it all.

It was healthy. And it was mostly fun. But it took work to make it happen consistently. It meant having a scheduled babysitter on Monday nights, which meant another line item in the budget. Was it worth it? Absolutely.

Be a Student of Your Spouse

We live in the age of the enneagram, temperament studies, personality assessments, and love languages. Being a student of other people has never been easier. And being a student of your spouse has never been more important.

Our first discovery of anything like this was when our small group read Dr. Gary Chapman's *The Five Love Languages.* It was life-changing—or maybe better, marriage-altering—for Andy and me.

It was a light-bulb moment to finally understand why my conquering of the to-do list often left him frustrated and feeling ignored. It was a breakthrough for him to wrap his head around the fact that sitting and talking in a restaurant until they started flicking the lights on and off was less than life-giving to me. When he understood that my love language is acts of service, or at least was during those heavy-duty parenting years, he got busy figuring out ways to help. When I realized quality time was important to him, I learned to put the distractions aside and give him my undivided attention.

But really. What makes *your* spouse feel loved? What lights him up? In what environment and circumstances do you see her come most alive? Figure it out, and make it your major.

What's her favorite candy or flower? Buy her some. Do words of affirmation and encouragement fill him up? Get yourself some notecards and leave them where you can see them so you'll remember to dole 'em out. Is there a family reunion coming up, and she's all about it but you'd rather have a root canal? Get excited about this opportunity to *love her well*, and work out all the details for the trip. Figure out your spouse and speak his love language. If it means putting reminders on your calendar or to-do list, so be it.

Be a student of your spouse, and act on what you learn.

Be Your Spouse's Loudest Cheerleader

It isn't your job to keep your spouse humble.

When Andy and I were newlyweds, we got into the habit of inviting older couples who had more life and marriage experience over for dinner. Not only was I a new wife, but I was also plunged directly from college student status to youth pastor's wife, seemingly without a clutch.

This particular evening, we were having dinner with an older couple who checked both boxes—they had a good number of marriage years under their belts *and* had been in ministry for a long time. As we talked and asked questions, the wife gave me some marriage advice.

She mentioned that her husband was a good communicator and people were always complimenting him. He received so many accolades at church, she was afraid he'd get a big head. So, being the thoughtful and dutiful wife, she appointed herself to keep him humble.

She shared a few examples of pointing out things he didn't do well. And she added that she would critique his sermons and share her valued insights on the way home from church.

I noticed he barely made eye contact with her while she talked about all this. By the time dinner was over, it was clear they did not have a super happy, fulfilling marriage. They didn't seem to hate each other, but it wasn't a relationship I wanted us to emulate.

I made a mental note that night not to be Andy's sermon critic. Ever.

Instead, I would be his greatest cheerleader.

This doesn't mean I'm not honest or that I don't share my thoughts at the appropriate time. But it *does* mean my goal is to build him up, not tear him down—publicly or privately.

As soon as I hear Andy's latest message, I tell him how *amazing* it was. I know I'm not the most objective because I still have quite a crush on him, but I do always think his messages are incredible. If I'm not with him, I text him and tell him how great it was and what I loved about it.

And don't even get me started on encouraging him when it's something outside his normal wheelhouse. When he wake-surfed for the first time, everyone within a ten-mile radius heard me cheering him on.

This works both ways in marriage. But, ladies, I think it's most powerful for us because, whether we like it or not, men seem more wired to crave honor, admiration, and affirmation, especially from us. So don't let anyone outcheer you. Be your spouse's loudest and greatest cheerleader.

While we're talking about it, let's not stop there. Take it a step further and be your spouse's most ardent defender.

We all love knowing someone is in our corner. They have our back. When our name comes up, they not only are quick to defend but lob in a compliment to boot.

Your words weigh a lot. Your compliments mean a lot. If you must err in one direction or the other, err on overcompliment-ing and overcheering. Err on not missing opportunities to build up your spouse—when they're present and when they're not.

Recently Allie reminded me of something I used to do

when I hung up the phone after talking to Andy. Whenever the kids were within earshot, I would hang up the phone and say, "I love that man."

The first time I said it was in our minivan while driving down the road with all three kids in the back. Andy had said something sweet, I'm sure, and when I pressed End Call, I spontaneously said, "I love that man." Something about saying it out loud to the kids, without Andy there, felt honoring. And it was true.

I decided to make it a habit. From that time on, whenever they were nearby, I hung up the phone and said those words.

Looking back, I think it was purposeful and powerful on several levels. It honored Andy in his absence. It gave our kids added security that in a world where friends' parents were frequently splitting up, their parents were okay. And it was a constant reminder that I really do love that man. And it's okay to show it.

Practice Showing Gratitude

Andy and I thank each other for stuff all the time. It's a habit and it's a good one.

When we first married, we didn't divvy up the chore list. Somehow we gravitated to doing certain things, and those things evolved into the weight we each pull. We were raised similarly, so maybe for us it didn't require a conversation. Your situation might be different.

Andy has typically been the trash guy. Don't read anything

into that. I just mean trash-trash. He notices when the trash cans are getting full, and he takes care of them. If I'm around when he does it, I always thank him. I thank him for noticing, or I thank him for always doing it. Or I mention how particularly stinky it was, so, "Thank for you sparing me." I'm grateful and I show it.

I cook. I like to cook. It's my way to be creative and make things pretty. Healthy living is my hobby, and cooking is the primary outlet for that. So I cook.

Andy doesn't cook. If I'm out of town, I know he'll have a peanut butter and jelly sandwich *every single day*. Unless he's in the car and sees a Chick-fil-A.

But he for sure will *not* cook. He's grateful that I do. And he thanks me all the time. He says, "Wow, this looks amazing," even when it doesn't. He whips out his phone to take a picture if it does happen to look special. He doesn't take it for granted, and he makes me feel appreciated for the effort.

In marriage, like in parenting or managing, what's rewarded is repeated. It feels good to be appreciated, to get credit for our work, and to be noticed for what we do and who we are. So when we're praised for our work, even with simple words of gratitude, we're far more likely to repeat it.

The flip side?

Unexpressed gratitude communicates ingratitude, whether we mean for it to or not.

"Well, that's his job," doesn't cut it. Neither does, "She loves doing that, so why should I thank her?" Err on the side of overthanking. If it gets on their nerves a bit, you can dial it back. But find the sweet spot of regularly expressing gratitude to your spouse.

Harness the "Aah Factor"

I wish I could remember where we heard about the "aah factor." We didn't make it up. I'm pretty sure it was a buried gem within a book we read in our small group. Initially it sounded kind of corny to us. But Andy and I latched on to it, maybe at first just to make fun of it.

Until we realized its impact.

The aah factor is the look of happiness that spreads across someone's face when the person they love walks into a room. It's the positive feeling someone experiences when they hear the garage door rise as their loved one gets home from work. It's the noticeable intake of breath when a person makes an appearance all dressed up and ready to go out. When I walk into the green room on a Sunday morning and Andy's face lights up in front of his coworkers? That's the aah factor.

But the aah factor is more than a feeling. It's also the practiced expression of it. I can be happy about Andy getting home from work, but when I meet him at the door and tell him how much I love hearing the garage door rise up because that means he's about to walk in, that's harnessing the power of the aah factor.

After many years of marriage, the aah factor still hits the mark.

It honors. It strengthens. It communicates the powerful notion of "I'd choose you all over again." It's something we can practice and make a habit. It's a powerful way of investing in our most important human relationship. And it's one of the things that got us to the empty nest years still liking each other a lot.

I'll readily admit that the aah factor comes easily during those early, infatuation years when pausing and appreciating happen without thought. Then life happens. We get busy. We get distracted. Feelings erode.

Perhaps you're rolling your eyes and thinking, "That's great for you and Andy. Congratulations and all. But I'm not feeling any aah when *our* garage door goes up. More like *ugh*."

May I suggest giving it a try?

Aah always starts somewhere. And aah always starts with someone. You may have more control over aah and ugh than you think.

I remember sharing this idea with a girlfriend who wasn't feeling much "aah." She literally rolled her eyes and told me it would never work.

But she tried it. Several times.

While it might not have revolutionized their entire marriage in a few tries, it was part of a package of things that began making a difference.

So give it some thought and maybe take a stab at harnessing the aah factor. Let me know what you think.

Conclusion

Set your kids up well.

> Prioritize and invest.
> Be a student of your spouse.
> Be your spouse's loudest cheerleader.
> Practice showing gratitude.
> Harness the "aah factor."

A healthy marriage is not a perfect marriage. It's not a relationship where conflict, struggle, and grief are absent. Rather, it's a relationship where mutual respect and mutual submission are the identified goals—even amid that conflict, struggle, or grief.

As Andy has taught for years, mutual submission is a race to the back of the line. It's a "you first" posture that fosters a climate of selflessness.

That selflessness preserves and protects the relationship in the short term, thus giving our kids security now. But it also casts a vision for our kids' future marriages. It gives them a healthy benchmark of expectations and a leg up in their own future marriages and families.

So let's get this marriage thing right. Let's get it right for us and for the futures of our marriages. And let's get it right for the futures of our kids. Let's give 'em a great story to tell.

CHAPTER 10

Spiritual Formation

(ANDY)

Regarding the faith of our children, the *win*, or the *it*, was for each of them to develop a faith of their own. Specifically, we wanted them to develop a *Christian* faith of their own.

We wanted our kids to acknowledge and embrace a sense of personal accountability to their heavenly Father as early as possible. Then, as they got older, our hope was that they would actively follow Jesus. These simple wins clarified and defined our role in the process.

The win wasn't Bible scholars, so we didn't conduct in-depth Bible studies. On the other end of the spectrum, the win wasn't simply for our children to become Christians. So the finish line wasn't a salvation prayer and baptism. Our desire was for each of our children to have an active personal faith of their own that matured as they matured. With that in mind, our role was pretty straightforward: *to inspire and equip our children to trust God and follow Jesus.*

We did a variety of things through the years to facilitate this outcome. Rather than list everything we did, we'll focus on the few things our kids say made the biggest difference. But before that, this.

Predecide

When you consider the faith of your children, what's the win? The finish line? What are you hoping and praying for? These are important questions because . . .

> Your *win* will determine your *role* in the development of your children's faith.

Or it should, anyway.

For many Christian parents, the *win* is to get 'em *in*—namely, to ensure their children end up in heaven someday. Put another way, the win is to eternity-proof their kids. When that's the goal, the parents' role is reduced to ensuring their kids dot all the salvation i's and cross all the salvation t's in accordance with their faith tradition—catechism, baptism, recite a prayer, First Communion—all of which usually happen before kids are even old enough to have a genuine faith of their own. Once the kids are *in*, Mom and Dad's role comes to an end. But in many instances, their children's faith comes to an early end as well.

Heaven-someday faith is easy to deconstruct and abandon.

Heaven-someday faith rarely survives the rigors, distractions, and disappointments of young adulthood. When a son or daughter walks away from their heaven-someday brand of faith, Christian parents are understandably distraught. But often they are unwitting accomplices in the undermining of their children's faith. Here's why I say that: as it relates to the endurance of your child's faith, what happens at *home* is far more catalytic than what happens at *church*.

What happens at home is more catalytic than your child's baptism, sinner's prayer, or catechism. If your faith doesn't make a practical difference in *your* life, odds are your kids will grow indifferent toward all things religious. If believing doesn't impact living, why believe? That only amounts to needless guilt. Who has time for that?

Somebody who's *not* you can teach your children the books of the Bible and the stories contained within them. But only you can demonstrate day by day, season by season what it looks like to allow the teaching of Jesus to shape decisions and relationships. Nobody has a better opportunity than you to model for your children the sustaining power of faith in God during difficult times. For the record, heaven-someday faith is not the version of faith Jesus taught or modeled. He taught and modeled a "follow me" version.

So when it comes to the faith of your children, what's the win? Heaven someday? Or practical, enduring faith every day? If you hope to provide your children with an enduring, robust, real-world faith of their own, you have an ongoing role to play.

Relational Faith

As I mentioned a few paragraphs ago, we did a variety of things through the years to help our children develop an enduring faith of their own. The following are the things our kids said made the biggest impact.

1. We emphasized a personal relationship with God.

One of the first prayers we taught our children was this:

> Dear heavenly Father, please show me your will for my life.

This was one of the first prayers my dad taught me as well. He would say, "Andy, God has a plan for your life, and you don't want to miss it." I certainly did not. Teaching me that simple prayer was my father's way of introducing me to the idea that my first line of accountability was to my Father in heaven. The habit of praying this simple prayer every night before I went to sleep had a profound impact on my sister and me. So every night I would conclude my bedtime prayer routine with, ". . . and please show me your will for my life. Amen."

Unfortunately, during that same season, my parents introduced me to the disturbing piece of narrative from the Old Testament when God speaks audibly to young Samuel in the middle of the night. Familiar with that story? If not, here's a quick recap. Hannah had trouble getting pregnant. She and her husband, Elkanah, had tried for years, to no avail. But Elkanah had two wives. Adding insult to injury, Peninnah, wife number two, had no trouble getting pregnant. So Hannah was greatly distressed. In her desperation, she vowed to God that if he gave her a son, she would give him back to serve in whatever manner God saw fit. In time, God granted her request. She had a baby boy and named him Samuel. And true to her vow, she took him to the prophet Eli and left him there to serve God alongside the aging prophet.

So far, so good.

Then one night young Samuel hears a voice calling his name. He assumes it's Eli, so he runs to Eli's bedside. Turns out it wasn't Eli. This happens two more times. Eli realizes something is up and tells Samuel that if he hears the voice again he should respond, "Speak, LORD, for your servant is listening."[2] Sure enough, it was the voice of God. And God gives Samuel a glimpse into his will for Samuel's life.

The moral of the story, according to my parents, anyway, was to be listening on the off chance that God chose to speak to me the way he did to little Samuel. And if so, I was to respond as Samuel did. However, I'm confident if God, or anyone for that matter, whispered my name in the middle of the night, my parents would have had to change my sheets in the middle of that same night. Theirs as well. I most certainly would have spent the rest of the night sandwiched between them.

In spite of all that, I continued to ask God to show me his will throughout my life.

If I'm honest, sometimes I hoped God was busy showing somebody else his will for their life, because I had a pretty good idea of what I wanted to do with mine. And I was confident our wills didn't line up. But even then I continued to ask God to show me his will. This simple habit kept me looking up and looking ahead. It provided me with a sense of destiny. If God had a will or plan for my life, I didn't want to miss it. If God had a plan for my life, what could possibly be more important?

So it's no surprise this was one of the first prayers we taught our children to pray. And as I did, they tacked it on to the end of their nightly prayers: ". . . and please show me your will for my life. Amen."

And no, I did not use the story of little Samuel as a selling point.

People of faith have long debated whether God has a specific plan for each individual. A case can be made for both sides of that debate. But at sixty-four, I still ask God to show me his will. You'd think I'd know his will by now, right? So why ask? For the same reason I've always asked: it keeps me looking up and looking ahead.

Garrett, our middle child, is twenty-eight and married. Recently, he and his wife, Danielle, went to look at a house for sale in a neighborhood they've had their eye on. The good news was they loved the house. The bad news was there were four full-price offers in the queue. On their way home they called Sandra to chat about it. Sandra mentioned that she and I were willing to make it possible for them to make an all-cash offer, pretty much ensuring the owner would accept their offer.

I hope Dave Ramsey isn't reading this.

Garrett called Sandra back a few minutes later. "Mom," he said, "that is so generous of you and Dad. But we feel like that removes the faith element for us. And I don't want to eliminate the opportunity for God to close the door." Translated: We want God's will for our lives more than we want this house.

That's *it*.

But as it turned out, that house wasn't it.

Directing your children's attention to God's will for their lives is an important first step in helping them develop a relationship *with* their heavenly Father and accountability *to* their heavenly Father. Once that relationship is in place, look for opportunities *not* to make decisions for your children, and encourage them to look to their Father in heaven for guidance. In this way, you help them develop the habit of looking up, not just over, for direction.

My parents modeled this so well. When I was in the eleventh grade, Elton John came to town. I wanted to be Elton at the time. Just so you know, my dad did *not* want me to be Elton John. The concert was scheduled for a Sunday night. We went to church on Sunday nights. Every Sunday night. So I assumed I knew the answer to my question before I asked it, but I asked anyway: "Dad, Elton John is coming to the Omni. I really want to go. But it's on a Sunday night." To my amazement he responded, "Well, why don't you pray about it, and whatever you think the Lord would have you do, that'll be fine."

All these years later, his response is still a bit hard to fathom. The church world was different then. My dad was putting a bit of his reputation on the line by leaving that decision in my court. If I went, everybody at church would know. But he said to pray about it, so I did. I didn't hear anything from God, so I interpreted his silence as a green light. I purchased four tickets: one for me, one for Louie Giglio, and two more for two additional church friends whose parents eventually succumbed to, "Dr. Stanley is letting Andy go!"

Off we went in my mom's beige four-door Catalina. Later my parents told me they prayed I would be miserable the entire night. God did not answer their prayer. At the end of the night, I still wanted to be Elton John and marry somebody who looked like Kiki Dee.

Oh well.

The moral of the story is that giving your children the running room necessary to develop a faith of their own doesn't come without risks. But I'm convinced it's much riskier to send them off to college without a sense of personal accountability to their heavenly Father. So start early.

We did.

For example . . .

Andrew and Garrett played baseball year-round from the time they were ten through high school—the very thing college and professional athletes recommend kids *not* do.

But Sandra and I enjoyed it.

Andrew was eleven the first time a baseball tournament interfered with church. When the coach announced what time we would need to be at the ballpark the following Sunday morning, Andrew immediately turned to look at me. He was thinking the same thing he *thought* I was thinking: "What about church!" The truth is, I was thinking, "I wonder who I can get to preach for me Sunday so I don't miss the tournament?"

Our secret.

On the way home he said, "Dad, what should I do?" I told him Sunday was the Sabbath and that he should keep it holy! That's how you raise kids with the *Bible* in mind.

Actually, I told Andrew it was up to him. I told him to pray about it and whatever he thought he should do, that's what we would do. That was on a Friday. The next morning he told me he thought God wanted him to play. So he did.

Turns out, God wanted me to preach.

So I did.

Moving on.

2. We taught our children to pay attention to their hearts.

The Old Testament book of Proverbs is filled with extraordinary wisdom. Most of it is as practical today as it was when the collection was originally assembled. That so much good advice is packed into this ancient document is all the more reason the following statement should cause us to sit up straight and pay attention:

Above *all* else . . .

Implication: If you forget everything else written in this collection of sayings, don't forget this.

> Above all else, guard *your heart*,

Not our wallets? Our purses? Our daughters? Why "our hearts"? And why "above all else"?

> for everything you *do* flows from it.[3]

Think about that. Everything we do on the outside originates on the inside. If that's true, then by all means we should pay attention to what's going on inside. Jesus agreed. His version went like this:

> Out of the heart come evil thoughts—murder, adultery, sexual immorality, theft, false testimony, slander.[4]

That's quite a list. Any one of those behaviors has the potential to put us down for the count. And according to Jesus they originate in our hearts. They come from within. That being the case, we would do well to guard our hearts. The problem is, no one taught us how to do that. Our entire lives we've been encouraged to monitor our behavior. But if Jesus is correct, guarding our *hearts* may be more important than monitoring our *behavior*. The Old Testament book of Proverbs is filled with guidance related to behavior. But at the same time, it instructs readers to get in the habit of paying attention to what's swirling around on the inside, because what's on the inside doesn't stay there. Our hearts direct our behavior.

Since this is a book about *parenting*, not *adulting*, I'll let you decide what to do about *your* heart. But what about your children's hearts?

You spend a good deal of time teaching your children to monitor their behavior. But what about guarding their hearts? Have you taught your children how to do that? If it's "above all else," if everything they do originates there, teaching your kids to guard their hearts should be a priority.

We certainly thought so.

We thought so, but we weren't sure how.

One evening as I was putting Andrew to bed, I decided to take the direct route. Andrew was probably six years old at the time. We had already prayed and were chatting about the events of the day. Right before I got up to leave, I put my hand on his chest and said, "Andrew, is everything okay in your heart?" As soon as I did, I thought, "Lighten up, Dad. He's just a kid!"

Andrew smiled and said, "Yes, sir, Daddy." That became a bedtime routine I eventually did with all three of our children. I decided the first step to guarding their hearts was to help them get in the habit of paying attention to what was going on in there. Over time I added several other questions. Eventually the list looked like this:

- Is everything okay in your heart?
- Did anybody hurt your feelings today?
- Are you mad at anybody?
- Are you worried about anything?

- Did anybody break a promise to you today?
- Is there anything you want to tell me but you're not
  sure how?

One night I was working through my list with Allie, and for some reason I added, "Is there anybody whose failure you would secretly celebrate?" She was so young at the time, I wasn't sure she would understand the question. Her response shocked me. She immediately blurted out a name. Fortunately, it wasn't one of her brothers. But it was one of her brother's friends. I said, "Allie, do you know what that question means?" She said, "Yes, sir, Daddy. It means if they didn't do good at something, I would be happy about it." Turns out she had something lodged in her heart that needed unlodging. So every once in a while, I would toss that question into the mix.

This was our routine for years. These questions became so ingrained that one night as I was putting Allie to bed, she lay down, closed her eyes, and said, "Daddy, everything is okay in my heart. Nobody hurt my feelings. I'm not mad at anybody. I'm not worried. And nobody broke a promise. Good night."

The questions we *most often* ask our children communicate what's *most important* to us and what we're convinced should be most important to them. As parents, we naturally gravitate toward questions about their behavior and performance: Did you brush your teeth? Did you finish your homework? Did you clean your room? How did you do on your test?

The good news is that when it comes to reinforcing good behavior and excellent performance, we have a lot of help—teachers, coaches, bosses, friends, neighbors, and grand-parents. But when it comes to equipping and motivating our kids to examine and guard their hearts, it's pretty much us or nobody. And the author of that statement from Proverbs isn't wrong. The condition of our children's hearts is *above all things* because their emotional health determines their relational health and, ultimately, their behavior and performance.

I'm sure you wonder at times if your teachable moment chats are *getting through* or if your kids just wait for you to *get through* so they can get back to what they want to do. We certainly wondered. I was in the middle of a particularly riveting life lesson during dinner one night when Garrett suddenly raised his hand. For the record, we didn't require our children to raise their hands at the dinner table. So I assumed this was something important.

"Yes, Garrett?"

"Dad, you have mustard on your shirt."

"Thank you, Garrett. Everyone can be excused now."

But fortunately, every once in a while, a little light shines through to indicate that maybe we're getting through. On a different occasion, as we were finishing dinner, I mentioned that a friend of the family was sick again and that I thought this individual's physical challenges were caused by deeper issues. Andrew immediately latched on to that. "What's a deeper issue?" he asked.

This was someone they all knew, so I needed to be careful. But at the same time, it was a good opportunity to illustrate what can happen when someone doesn't guard their heart.

So I forged ahead. I explained the relationship between our physical health and the health of our hearts. I talked specifically about the danger of harboring secrets and how secrets can make you sick. Everybody seemed interested, so I kept going. I talked about how an incident in childhood could affect an adult later in life and how the adult often doesn't even remember the incident but is still affected. I concluded with, "This is why it's so important to pay attention to our hearts. And this is why it's so important that we confess our sins. Confession keeps unhealthy secrets from getting stuck in our hearts."

I'd barely gotten the last sentence out of my mouth when Garrett, who was nine at the time, said he needed to tell me something.

I said, "Okay."

He said, "Not here, Dad." Then he got up from the table and headed down the hall. I sent the other two kids upstairs and followed him to my study. Once he knew we were out of earshot from the rest of the family, Garrett proceeded to tell me about an incident that had happened at a neighbor's house. Something minor. But something that was stuck in his conscience.

"When did this happen?" I asked.

"A long time ago," he replied.

I thanked him for telling me, hugged him, and told him how proud I was that he'd cleared his conscience and cleaned out his heart.

About twenty minutes later, as Sandra and I were cleaning

up the kitchen, Garrett came downstairs and said, "Mom, can I talk to you for a minute?" She followed him down the hall and listened as he confessed the rest of the incident that he'd only partially confessed to me. She hugged him and told him how proud she was of his desire to clean out his heart. Back in the kitchen, we both commented on how great it was that he was learning the importance of confession at such a young age.

Little did we know.

At bedtime, the same night, Garrett asked if he could speak to Sandra alone. So I left the room. He proceeded to confess another incident he'd been feeling guilty about. This one wasn't quite as severe as the first.

An hour later, Sandra and I were working in our office when we heard footsteps coming down the hall. It was Garrett. "I feel like I need to tell you guys something, but I don't know what it is." I told him to go back to bed and then, when it was clear, to come back down and tell us. A few minutes later he was back. "I remember what it was." He told us about yet another minor incident we didn't know about.

At 10:30 p.m. Sandra and I were lying in bed, chuckling about Garrett's evening of confession, when we heard footsteps in the hall once more. Garrett again. He came over to my side of the bed. It took everything in me not to say, "What else?" But I refrained.

"Mom, Dad," he said, "yesterday when Allie wasn't here, I went into her room without asking."

I knew we'd reached the bottom of the confession barrel. Once again I thanked him for his honesty. I assured him God would honor his willingness to clean out his heart. He stood there for a moment. Then he smiled and said, "Well, I don't want to get sick!" Then he turned around and headed back up to his room.

I realize that sounds like a made-up preacher story, but that's exactly what happened. Garrett doesn't remember it. We'll never forget it. And I haven't even told you the best part. The next night, when we were saying our prayers with Garrett, he went through his normal prayer routine, but just before he said, "Amen," he paused and added, "And thank you that I have a clean heart."

That's *it*.

Teach your children to guard their hearts. Teach your kids how to clean out their hearts every day for the rest of their lives. You may not like our approach. That's fine. Like I said, we made it up. But our kids would tell you it made a difference.

3. We prayed together in every season.

Parents often pray with or for their children at night when putting them to bed. We certainly did. But our children say they appreciated that we continued to pray with them even after they were old enough to put themselves to bed. We prayed together as a family from the childhood years through the high school years. While our kids didn't always appreciate it then, they do now.

In the early years, prayer time was also an opportunity to help our children memorize several passages of

Scripture—Scripture we then taught them to incorporate into their prayers. We began with the Lord's Prayer.[5] After all, Jesus is quoted as saying,

> This, then, is how you should pray . . . [6]

So we decided that was how we should pray.

Then we helped our children memorize several other short passages of Scripture. These three passages from Psalms and Proverbs were some of the earliest:

> How blessed is the man who does not walk in
> >the counsel of the wicked,
> Nor stand in the path of sinners,
> Nor sit in the seat of scoffers!
> But his delight is in the law of the LORD,
> And in His law he meditates day and night.
> He will be like a tree firmly planted by streams
> >of water,
> Which yields its fruit in its season
> And its leaf does not wither;
> And in whatever he does, he prospers.[7]

> How can a young man keep his way pure?
> By keeping it according to Your word.
> With all my heart I have sought You;
> Do not let me wander from Your
> >commandments.

Your word I have treasured in my heart,
That I may not sin against You.[8]

The prudent see danger and take refuge,
    but the simple keep going and pay the penalty.[9]

Just for fun, I also had my boys memorize David's speech to Goliath moments before the boy took down the giant. Not only did they memorize it, they also would stand on their beds and channel their best shepherd, boy-warrior David.

You come against me with sword and spear and javelin, but I come against you in the name of the Lord Almighty, the God of the armies of Israel, whom you have defied. This day the Lord will deliver you into my hands, and I'll strike you down and cut off your head. This very day I will give the carcasses of the Philistine army to the birds and the wild animals, and the whole world will know that there is a God in Israel. All those gathered here will know that it is not by sword or spear that the Lord saves; for the battle is the Lord's, and he will give all of you into our hands.[10]

This was more than an exercise in Scripture memory. As I mentioned earlier, we helped our children incorporate bits and pieces of these ancient but relevant passages into their prayers. Hiding God's Word in our children's hearts takes many forms. This is one we chose when they were young.

In addition to phrases from Scripture and the request that God would show them his will for their lives, we taught our children one other prescripted prayer.

Give me the wisdom to know what's right and the courage to do what's right even when it's hard.

This is something Sandra and I have prayed consistently for ourselves *and* with our kids. Of all the things we taught our children to pray, this one aged well as they aged.

When our children were young, we usually gathered in Allie's room to pray. Sandra and I knelt by the bed, the kids laid on their stomachs facing us, and we all took turns praying. This worked until the boys hit middle school. At that point Allie insisted we move prayer time out of her room because inevitably one of the boys would pass gas, which not only interrupted prayer time but also left a not so gentle reminder of the boys' presence in her room. That's when we instituted "stair prayer."

It's exactly what it sounds like. We met on the stairs (neutral territory) for prayer. Most every night around eight o'clock, we'd tell the kids to stop whatever they were doing for stair prayer. On some nights I prayed a short prayer and released everybody back to their homework. On other nights we all prayed. Occasionally, these impromptu gatherings turned into extended discussions about something going on with a member of our family or with one of the kids' friends. We continued stair prayer until our youngest, Allie, graduated from high school and left home for college.

Now, if you're picturing the holy Stanley family gathered reverently on our staircase while interceding on behalf of one another and the world, you have the wrong picture.

Case in point: One evening I decided to try something new, a strategy that always worked with our adult small group. "Kids," I said, "tonight I want you to pray for the person to your right." All three kids immediately jumped up and tried to squeeze between Sandra and me so they didn't have to pray for each other. I made 'em sit back down, said a short prayer, and sent everybody to their rooms.

Feel better now?

As chaotic as it was at times, stair prayer is one of the things our kids remember and are most grateful for.

4. We were open about our own faith journeys.

For our children to have a faith of their own, it's imperative they understand how faith intersects with the real world.

Their world in particular.

Literal Goliaths? Probably not. But fear, relational conflict, temptation, rejection, loneliness, anxiety, failure, disappointment, peer pressure? Those are their twenty-first-century Goliaths, just to name a few. Those are examples of the "even when it's hard" part of the wisdom prayer mentioned earlier.

In light of that, we always looked for opportunities to talk about how our personal faith informed or should have informed our actions and reactions to real-world current events and relationships. We were intentional and, of course, age appropriate with what we shared. As our kids entered middle school and high school, we pulled out a few stories from our past that we'd been saving for the right time.

When Allie entered middle school, Sandra shared two faith-defining stories she hadn't told before. One involved a breakup, the other a modeling opportunity she turned down because it conflicted with her faith-informed values. When our kids were in high school, I asked them to read chapter 2 of my book *Deep & Wide*, where I recount the events surrounding my not so smooth transition from working for my dad to wondering what was next, a decision that eventually led to the establishment of North Point Community Church.

The point being, we wanted our children to understand what it looks and feels like when faith intersects with real-time, real-world circumstances. We wanted them to know that following Jesus has implications for everything and everybody, that our faith should inform both our actions and our *reactions*. After all, our reactions say more about the sincerity and depth of our faith than anything else. We talked about how much money we gave away and why. We were (appropriately) open about challenges with friends and work associates. No surprise, being open made it easier for them to be open as well. And on a handful of memorable occasions, our kids were quick to remind us of what we were constantly reminding them.

In the spirit of transparency, we didn't limit the stories to *our* stories. We discussed other people's faith journeys and lack-of-faith journeys as well. As Vernon Law famously stated, "Experience is a hard teacher because she gives the test first, the lesson afterward." Our children will be forced to learn some things the hard way. But the hard way is often measured in years and tears. If it can be avoided, it should be. And if our kids can learn from the experience of others, all the better. It's why we recounted a few not so stellar moments from our pasts to head our kids off at the pass.

My day job provided me an advantage in the learn-from-the-mistakes-of-others department. I get a lot of email from people who learned the hard way and write to tell me about it. So on occasion I would print an email or two and read them at the dinner table. I would always conclude with, "That's what sin will do to you, kids!"

Not really.

But close.

Let's be honest. As parents, we rarely miss an opportunity to point out when our kids aren't getting it right. But those moments are in the moment. They are personal and emotional. On the other hand, stories illustrate outcomes of faithfulness and unfaithfulness in the broader, cause-and-effect context of life. Stories remind our children that today's actions have consequences tomorrow. That all of life is, in fact, connected.

Last but not least . . .

5. We kept our children engaged with our church.

When parents ask me, "Should I make my kids attend church?" my initial response is, "You shouldn't have to *make* your kids go to church. They should want to go. If they don't want to go, you may need to find another church."

If your church isn't helping you become a better parent and equipping your kids to develop a faith of their own, find another church.

I'll wait.

Seriously. If you raise your children in a church that leaves them with the impression that faith is irrelevant in the real world, more than likely they will leave your faith in exchange for the real world. I can't tell you how many parents of middle school and high school students pulled Sandra and me aside at the ballpark or gymnastics practice to ask if our church had a "good program" for teenagers. We did. And I assured them we did. But I did not tell them what I was thinking. I was thinking, "You should have had your children in a good church when they were five rather than waiting until they were fifteen." If you've raised teenagers, you understand.

By the time Mom and Dad realize there's a problem, the problem has been a problem for quite some time. So get your children plugged into a local church that is committed to part-nering with you to equip your kids to develop a faith of their own. And yes, there may be times when you will have to insist they attend. But you insist they attend school, right? So make church a priority. Make the *right* church a priority. If you do, you and your kids will have the benefit of another adult or two reiterating at church what you're modeling and teaching at home.

One More (Big) Thing

These are the five things our kids said made the biggest difference in helping them develop and maintain a faith of their own:

1. We emphasized a personal relationship with God.
2. We taught our children to pay attention to their hearts.
3. We prayed together in every season.
4. We were open about our own faith journeys.
5. We kept our children engaged with our church.

While those five practices equipped our children to develop a faith of their own, those practices were taught through a specific faith framework.

Actually, everything we've discussed throughout this book was filtered through and informed by a specific faith or theological framework. As Sandra and I wrestled with how to conclude this book, we agreed that we would be remiss and perhaps even misleading if we failed to share it with you.

CHAPTER 11

This Is *It*

(ANDY)

Mom, Dad, I don't believe anymore."

These are words no Christian parent wants or expects to hear. These are words no parent of *any* faith system who has endeavored to pass along their faith to their children wants to hear.

It's devastating. It's personal. It's a parenting fail of the first order.

Sure, they can read and write and have above-average SAT scores. But if a child walks away from faith? That's a loss difficult to compensate for with traditional parenting wins. When kids second-guess their faith, parents often second-guess their parenting: What did we do wrong? Should we have sent her to Christian school? Did the Christian school undermine his Christian faith? Should we have attended a different church?

Why our kids and not theirs? Why him but not his brother or sister?

Andrew, our oldest, was our only child (so far) to lose faith. Fortunately it was temporary. He told me first. I told Sandra. She was terrified. When Sandra is terrified, it's my fault even when it isn't.

Over the years, we've discovered several rat snakes in our yard, some quite large, which explains why we've never seen any rats. I say *we've* discovered. Actually, *Sandra* is always the first to discover snakes. And she hates snakes. Considering her reaction, you might conclude I bring the snakes home and strategically place them to ensure she is the first to encounter them. She admits that blaming me is irrational. But it's where she goes. So I always take responsibility, which requires a measure of creativity. When I struggle to connect the fault-dots, I default to, "It's my fault, honey. If I hadn't asked you to marry me to begin with, this never would have happened."

Anyway.

When I told Sandra that Andrew didn't think he believed in God anymore, she immediately wanted to know what I was going to do about it. I smiled and reassured her, "He'll be fine."

I'm not sure why that wasn't reassuring.

To her, "He'll be fine" sounded a lot like, "Don't worry; I don't plan to do anything about this." Which was true. I wasn't planning to do anything about it because Andrew was seven years old at the time. Honestly, I was relieved he deconverted early so we could get it out of the way. It gave us plenty of time to reconvert him, hopefully before he reached the *age of accountability*, something Protestants invented.

So I wasn't worried. But Sandra was. Turns out she didn't need to be. And she would tell you I got this one right. I didn't pressure Andrew. I didn't ask *why*. But I did ask *when*. However, he wasn't sure when it started. I also asked him if it was okay to continue praying with him at night. He assured me it was. During that season I didn't insist that he pray. Then once or twice a week, I would ask him, "Andrew, how's your faith?"

This went on for several months. I went out of my way not to pressure him or even talk about it unless he brought it up. Then one night while I was getting him ready for bed, he said, "Dad, I think I have my faith back."

So I said to my servants, "Quick! Bring the best robe and put it on him. Put a ring on his finger and sandals on his feet. Bring the fattened calf and kill it. Let's have a feast and celebrate. For this son of mine was dead and is alive again; he was lost and is found."

Actually, I said, "That's great, Andrew. I'm so glad we can talk about stuff like that. Do you want me to tell Mom, or do you want to tell her?" He let me tell her.

She was so relieved, she ran upstairs and threw Andrew over her shoulder and called our friends and neighbors and said, "Rejoice with me! I have found my lost sheep!"

Well, that's what she wanted to do. But she knew better. Remember, don't freak out. Freak out and your kids will shut down.

Good for You

If your initial response is, "Good for you, Andy, but my situation is different," I get it. It's different because your seventeen-year-old daughter has a *new* boyfriend who convinced her to abandon her *old* faith. Or your nineteen-year-old son came home from college with a new tattoo and a new worldview. It's late in the game for you. Worse, it's mind-boggling. Infuriating. You spent seventeen-plus years teaching, modeling, exposing your kids to, and reinforcing a faith-centered worldview, and one cute guy later, one semester away from home later, it all evaporated. How can that be?

What could you have done to prevent it? What should you do now?

Much has been written on the topic of how and why young adults lose faith, so I won't attempt to tackle that here. I would have to know your entire story to comment on what you could have done to prevent it. But I can tell you what to do now. And for those of you with little ones still crawling or running around, this goes for you as well.

Parent with the relationship in mind.

That's still *it*.

Parent with the relationship, not their faith, in mind. Do everything in your power to keep your side of the relational drawbridge down, regardless of what they believe or don't believe and—and this is difficult—regardless of how they choose to live. Dare I take it a step further, maybe too much further?

Don't let *your faith* get in the way of *your relation-ships* with your children.

Now you know why we saved this for the last chapter.

If you're a Christian and your faith is getting in the way of your relationship with your children, you may have subscribed to the wrong version of your faith.

Here's why I say that: Jesus never allowed what he believed to separate him from people. Just the opposite. His perfect understanding of what God is like and who God likes compelled him to always keep his side of the relational drawbridge down with all kinds of people. Jesus liked people who were nothing like him, and they liked him back. They liked him back because they were convinced he *liked* them, which was *un*like other religious folks they knew.

The folks Jesus was constantly at odds with were religious folk who refused to follow his example. So, again, if your version of the Christian faith is or ever becomes an obstacle to your relationship with your children, you may have the wrong version. If your child walks away from your faith, it may break your heart. But as far as it depends on you, it should not break the relationship. Follow Jesus through the Gospels and that becomes abundantly clear.

I see that hand.

"But if I don't confront their sin and object to their behavior, won't it appear as if I condone it? Don't I become complicit? Don't I become guilty by association?"

Good questions.

Let's tackle the last one first. If Jesus were concerned about guilt by association, he would have stayed in heaven. So don't worry about that. If you're more worried about what your friends at church or your nosy neighbors think than how your children feel, that's on you. Don't parent your children with other people's opinions in mind. Or your reputation in mind. Besides, friends and neighbors come and go.

When it comes to confronting your child's error or lifestyle choices, remember this: Your child already knows what you believe and why you believe it. They already know what you condone and condemn. There's no need to go there. The more pressing issue is:

Do you know what *they* believe and *why* they believe it?

Remember chapter 1? *You are in a relationship with your children, but it is not the same relationship.* You are the parent. You're not the pastor. You're not the counselor. You're not an apologist. You're not an evangelist. The training years are behind you. Perhaps the coaching years are as well. Don't revert. Don't panic. Don't freak out. Be a student, not a critic. They aren't going to hell. They're just putting you through it.

So put your Bible and your apologetics books away and sit back down in your parent seat and be the parent. If your kids have moved out, these are the friendship years. Do you have friends whose values and lifestyle choices don't mirror yours? If so, you know what to do. If not, that may be part of the problem. Either way, find your parent seat and have a seat. And fasten your seat belt.

And pray.

But not for your wayward child. Not yet.

Pray for you.

Ask God to give you eyes to see your child the way he sees them. Is God afraid? Worried? Fretting? Freaking out? No. Pray that you would see as he sees and that you would respond as he responds. How does your heavenly Father respond to prodigal children? Jesus told us.

He puts out the welcome mat and waits.

He keeps his side of the drawbridge down. If Jesus was correct—and I, for one, think he was—God's side of the relational bridge doesn't even have cables or motors attached. It's always down.

Parenting with the relationship in mind positions you to navigate difficult discussions regarding faith with the relationship in mind as well. Why?

> Because parenting with the relationship in mind ensures that you lead with your *values* rather than your *beliefs*.

What do you value most about your children? Hopefully, the relationship. So if one or all of your children question or abandon *your* faith, continue to parent with the relationship in mind, because a healthy relationship keeps the door open and the drawbridge down.

Relationship equates to influence. Remember, never give up influence with your children unnecessarily. Or with anyone else, for that matter.

And just so you know, if your children lose their faith but then choose to return to faith, it won't be because you *convinced* them to. It won't be because you *convicted* them to. It won't be because you *coerced* or *controlled* them back. While these four Cs are often what we reach for first, they are relational kryptonite.

Don't believe me?

Do you feel comfortable with or look forward to a long car ride with adults who readily employ any of those four Cs in their relationship with you?

No.

You resist and avoid those folks. So don't become one of those folks.

Don't become one of those parents.

Leverage the four Cs with your middle schooler, high schooler, or college-age child and they will resist and avoid you. As noted earlier, you may be *right*, but you may *right* them *right* out the door. You may *right* them out of your life.

And that leads me to the point of this final chapter and, to some degree, the point of this entire book.

Jesus-Centric

If you reread the previous section from the beginning, you'll notice I anchored my argument to Jesus rather than the Bible. Quick review:

- Jesus never allowed what he believed to separate him from people.
- If Jesus were concerned about guilt by association, he would have stayed in heaven.
- Jesus liked people who were nothing like him, and they liked him back.
- How does your heavenly Father respond to prodigal children? Jesus clarified that. He puts out the welcome mat.

The foundation of the Christian faith is a person. To be a Christian is to be a partisan of or follower of Jesus. As you probably know, the term *Christ* is not a name. It's a title. It means "anointed one." Anointed as in anointed as king. Jesus is God's final king. This is why throughout the New Testament, Jesus is referred to as Lord, Christ, and King. All that to say, as Christians, we accept Jesus as our ultimate and final authority. He made his authority unmistakably clear minutes before he ascended into heaven:

> *All authority* in heaven and on earth has been given to me.[11]

On the evening before his crucifixion, King Jesus used his authority to establish a new covenant, or arrangement, between God and humanity.[12] While God's covenant with ancient Israel included hundreds of commands, Jesus's new covenant included only one:

A new command I give you: Love one another.
As I have loved you, so you must love one another. By
this everyone will know that you are my disciples, if
you love one another.[13]

Jesus's new-covenant command, to love as he loved us, is
to inform all our actions and reactions, including our actions
and reactions as parents. In other words, as followers of Jesus
we should take our parenting cues from him. He is our authority in all things. Including parenting.

And that's a good thing.

Through the years, Sandra and I have watched with broken
hearts as parents have attempted to raise their kids according to
the Bible. When the Bible itself is the foundation for parenting, everything in the Bible is available to parents as leverage.
Everything in the Bible is regarded as equally authoritative
and potentially applicable. At the same time, every Christian
parent who has attempted to raise their children according to
the Bible has adopted or created a filter that allows them to
ignore certain portions of the Old Testament. Christian parents don't feel obligated to stone their children even though
the Bible is clear that in some instances they should.[14]

When the Bible is viewed as a handbook for parents or
Christians in general, the teaching of Jesus is reduced to the
level of all the other teaching in the Bible. The story of Jesus
becomes just another Bible story. Jesus's new command, to
love as he loved us, becomes just one among hundreds of
biblical commands. But when you read the Gospels and the

book of Acts, that approach to the Christian faith is nowhere to be found.

Following his resurrection, Jesus was considered Lord and God. His words were considered *the word of God* because he was God incarnate, God in a body. If you want to know what God is like and who God likes, fix your eyes on Jesus. As the author of Hebrews reminds us, Jesus is the *author*, or leader, and the *perfecter* of our faith,[15] which is simply another way of saying Jesus is our authority.

Jesus came to reveal the Father in terms the world could finally understand. God *became* one of us to reveal himself *to* us. Everything that came before was a mere shadow of what was to come.[16] You can discover a bit about something from its shadow. But not everything. In Christ, God has revealed himself fully.

That being the case, the story of Jesus isn't merely a Bible story. It's *the* story. Jesus's new-covenant command isn't just one of many biblical commands. It's *the* command we are to prioritize our lives around. Loving one another as he loved us is our brand. It's what marks us as his followers.

New-Covenant Faith

The love-one-another-as-Jesus-loved-us version of faith is the one that informed our parenting. It's why we wanted our kids to acknowledge their personal accountability to their heavenly Father as early as possible. That was a first step toward learning to follow Jesus. It's why our win wasn't to raise Bible scholars.

It's why the finish line wasn't a salvation prayer. It's why our rules were few and our discipline centered on relationship restoration. Jesus had one rule and came to restore the human race to the Father. It's why we adopted a posture of *Oh no!* when our kids broke the rules or dishonored someone. That was Jesus's response to sin. Sin broke his heart because sin breaks people. Pretty much everything in the preceding chapters reflects our best attempt to follow Jesus in our role as parents.

Are you wondering if this really matters?

It does.

Earlier in this chapter I wrote, "If you're a Christian and your faith is getting in the way of your relationship with your children, you may have subscribed to the wrong version of your faith." If you wondered what I meant by "the wrong version," now you know. The first-century version of our faith is what turned the world upside down. The others-first ethic that characterized the early church is why we have a Bible to begin with. Adopting a Jesus-centric faith is not only a big deal, it's *the* deal.

Going with You

There's no guarantee your children will always believe what you raised them to believe. What they choose to believe is beyond your control. What *is* in your control is your response. Your reaction. Your best response is to live your life in such a way that your kids never doubt *you* believe what you raised them to believe.

While Garrett reviewed the content of this chapter, he reminded me of something I told him during his college days. It's something I told all my kids. I told 'em if they chose to walk away from faith that I was going with them! That was my way of saying, *Regardless of what you believe or don't believe, it won't change anything about our relationship. If you think leaving your faith behind means leaving me behind, you're mistaken. I loved you before you believed anything.*

I bet you loved your children before they believed anything as well.

So you've got this.

Remain seated in the seat created just for you when your first child was born. The mom seat. The dad seat. Parent from there. Love them from there. Show your kids what it looks and sounds like to follow Jesus as a parent. Chances are, one day they'll be parents as well. When they bring your first grandbaby home from the hospital, what may still be a bit fuzzy now will be crystal clear then.

Relationship is everything.

Everything.

So do for and be for your kids what you want your kids to do for and be for the next generation. Parent with the relationship in mind. Parent in such a way that your kids will want to be with you and with each other even when they no longer have to be.

That's *it*.

Sandra's Tips for Kids and Quiet Times

Moms of kids in the coaching season often ask me for tips on how to help their children develop the habit of daily devotions or, to use the terminology Andy and I grew up with, a daily quiet time—time set aside for prayer and Scripture reading. This is an important topic. And it was important to us as well. Andy and I both developed the habit of a daily quiet time when we were in high school. But we didn't want to wait until our kids were teenagers before introducing this important routine.

As Andy mentioned earlier, our desire was for our children to develop a faith of their own. We knew from personal experience that nothing contributed to us owning our own faith more than our devotional lives. So we started 'em early. We did three things in particular:

- Modeled it
- Encouraged it
- Made it easy

Model It

It goes without saying, but I'll say it anyway. It will be difficult to help your children develop this habit if *you're* not in the habit. So you may need to begin there. But assuming you have a quiet time routine of some sort, make sure your children know about it. I made sure our kids knew when and where I had my quiet time. Andy and I are big proponents of having a consistent time and place. My place was a chair in our bedroom. My time was early in the morning.

The kids knew those early moments were Mommy's time alone with God and that unless it was an emergency, they shouldn't disturb me. This was a message in and of itself: *Kids, you're important. But you're not most important.* On the occasions when they would forget and come storming into the room, I would invite them to join me. I loved that they saw me with my Bible open and my journal close at hand. From time to time I would read them something from my journal or share something I had prayed specifically for them that day.

While your devotional life is personal, it doesn't need to remain private, especially when your kids are young. Let them catch you reading, praying, and journaling. As is the case with many facets of parenting, some things are more easily caught than taught. So if you want your children to develop a consistent devotional life, model it.

Encourage It

To *encourage* is to "inspire with courage."[17] You've been encouraging your children to do, attempt, and reattempt things since they were born. But as you may have discovered along the way, there is a fine line between encouraging and nagging. And one quickly transitions to the other when we don't see progress—as we ourselves measure progress.

While nagging often works in the moment, nagging is not an effective habit-development strategy. Nagging does not *inspire* because nagging doesn't trigger *desire*. Nagging triggers resistance—resistance to the very thing we want our children to do. And in some cases the thing they need to do.

Granted, there are areas where it doesn't matter if our children never develop an intrinsic desire to do what we need or want them to do. If the reason your middle schooler keeps her room clean is to keep you off her back, so be it. But when it comes to our children's devotional lives, it's vital that they develop a heartfelt desire to make this a habit. So in this arena, nagging won't do. You'll need to stick with encouragement. You'll need to *inspire*.

So we didn't nag. We encouraged. And on occasion we bribed. In our house, bribing was a perfectly acceptable form of "encouragement." Bribes are inspiring, right? During the middle school and high school years, it wasn't uncommon for me to send our kids a link to a sermon I wanted them to watch and digest. Along with the link I would add, "Watch this and write down three insights. Show 'em to me or Dad and we will reward you with a twenty-dollar bill!"

Worked every time.

Money talks. It certainly talks more persuasively than nagging. The point of that incentivized exercise was to help them experience the value of carving out time for self-directed, faith-oriented learning. Bottom line, look for opportunities to encourage and reward this valuable routine.

Make It Easy

When our children transitioned from cribs to big-boy and big-girl beds, we placed an age-appropriate Bible on their nightstand. These were picture Bibles that included short stories.

As each kid matured, we made sure the version of the Bible on their nightstand matured right along with them. From the beginning we used Easter as the time to introduce these upgrades.

Every Easter I included a devotional book or Bible in our children's Easter baskets. For us, Easter was the perfect time to give another push on the devotional life flywheel. Allie was a fan of journaling, so I always included a new journal. The boys loved sports, so during their high school years, I would include a biography of an athlete who was outspoken about their faith. I always scattered a few cool pens and highlighters in among the other goodies as well.

This was our way of making it easy. And our kids came to expect and look forward to these upgraded devotional tools. This family tradition served as a reminder that a habit of personal devotions was something Andy and I valued for ourselves and valued for the kids.

If the habit of personal devotions is something you desire to pass along to your children, model it, encourage it, and make it easy. Keep the conversations in the green zone, the encouragement zone. Take their personalities, temperaments, birth order, and maturity into account. Their approach may never mirror yours. That's okay. The win is for your children to understand how important this spiritual discipline is to you and to know you desire it for them too.

Tips for Each Stage of Parenting

Whether you're dealing with littles in the days-are-long-but-the-years-are-short stage or teenagers with raging hormones, here are a few tips we think might help.

The Discipline Years

1. **Look for short breaks.** When our kids were little, I was at home full-time, so the parenting gig felt constant. I had them in a Mother's Morning Out program at a church near our house. It was only a short break, but it provided necessary mental replenishment. Just knowing that on Tuesdays and Thursdays I'd have a few hours to myself was gold. The ability to run child-free errands, to go for a quick lunch with a girlfriend, or even to be home alone getting things done without interruptions was huge for an enneagram one with a penchant for accomplishing things.

2. **Find community.** If you're not in a small group, figure out how to fit that into your schedule. Shave off something

else to make space. Community—people around you in the same season of life who get it and care, reinforcements when you're feeling low, and some inner-circle folks to walk alongside you through the tough things of life—gives life.

3. **Take one day at a time.** Especially in the harder seasons of parenting. God gives us grace and mercy for today. He doesn't give us a week's worth or a month's worth. He promises to give it to us *as we need it.* When we prayerfully take one day at a time, making the best decisions we can on behalf of ourselves and our kids, God meets us with exactly what we need.

4. **Seek the joy.** For those of you who love the baby and littles stage, bask in it, take a lot of pictures, enjoy every minute—it goes by so fast. For those of you who don't find this season to be your favorite, look for the joys in it. Maybe jot them down when you can. Perhaps put a few little gems on a sticky note and place it somewhere visible to make you smile when you feel empty—like a little reset button. But don't miss the joys that are unique to this season.

The Training Years

1. **Decide *ahead of time* what your family's calendar can handle, and stick to it.** The temptation to let your kids try every single sport and activity will be a real one, even if you think it won't.

2. **Begin helping your kids understand money.** Earlier than they could completely understand it, we began teaching our kids principles of giving, saving, and spending. We had three labeled jars in their rooms—GIVE, SAVE, and SPEND. Anytime they received money for birthdays or earned money for chores, we made a big deal of using the jars to give them a visual of the principles we knew would serve them well long after the jar method was obsolete.

3. **Don't skimp on date night!** These are the years when life gets busy and the kids' schedules can overtake yours. Set up standing date nights if you can. I remember when the kids were barely old enough to stay home alone; we would slip out to the nearest coffee shop, grab lattes, and drive around within a short radius of our neighborhood, taking advantage of some uninterrupted catch-up time.

4. **Make prayer time a regular practice.** We talked about "stair prayer" in the Spiritual Formation chapter. Find some practices that become a part of your family's regular rhythm that helps their faith grow. Keep it short. Don't preach a sermon. But make it regular and meaningful for everyone. Also, if you have boys, just know that any gathering can turn into a wrestling match at the drop of a hat.

5. **Celebrate when they do something right.** As referenced earlier, our favorite thing to pray regularly with our kids was this: "Lord, give us the wisdom to know what's right and the courage to do what's right even when

it's hard." Anytime you see your kids apply this, even if they aren't aware they're applying it, point it out and celebrate it like crazy. "Gosh, I'm so proud of you. That's that thing we've been praying. You knew what was right, and you did it even though it was hard."

The Coaching Years

1. **Don't resolve your kids' problems.** Resist rescuing when they're facing something hard. Coach. There's a reason coaches are penalized when they don't remain on the sidelines.

2. **Assure your kids you share the same goal: freedom.** You don't want their first year away from home to be the first year they have freedom to make decisions for themselves. We started with small freedoms early, and with demonstrated responsibility, those freedoms increased.

3. **Sometimes coaches need coaching.** Don't be afraid to ask for help or find someone a few years ahead of where you are in the parenting journey. Taking advantage of not having to learn everything the hard way is smart!

4. **Stay engaged with a local church.** As mentioned in chapter 10, partnering in your parenting journey with a great student ministry reinforces what you're likely trying to teach at home. Often our kids hear what a small group leader tells them even when they can't seem to hear it from us. I can remember, more than once, one of our kids coming home and sharing something their small group

leader told them that was life-changing. As they talked, everything in me wanted to say, "Yeah, like I've been saying for the last three years?" But I refrained and nodded, saying, "Wow. That's amazing. What a great insight."

The Friendship Years

1. Enjoy!

Notes

1. "Unmarried Childbearing," Centers for Disease Control and Prevention, last reviewed May 16, 2022, https://www.cdc.gov/nchs/fastats/unmarried-childbearing.htm.
2. 1 Samuel 3:9.
3. Proverbs 4:23, italics added.
4. Matthew 15:19.
5. See Matthew 6:9–13.
6. Matthew 6:9.
7. Psalm 1:1–3 (NASB 1995).
8. Psalm 119:9–11 (NASB 1995).
9. Proverbs 22:3.
10. 1 Samuel 17:45–47.
11. Matthew 28:18, italics added.
12. See Luke 22:20.
13. John 13:34–35.
14. See Deuteronomy 21:18–21 and Exodus 21:17.
15. See Hebrews 12:2.
16. See Colossians 2:17.
17. *Merriam-Webster*, s.v. "encourage (*v.*)," accessed June 17, 2022, https://www.merriam-webster.com/dictionary/encourage.

Parenting Bible Study Guide plus Streaming Video

Getting It Right

Andy and Sandra Stanley

Also available from Andy and Sandra:
6-Session Parenting Video Series

Available in stores and online!

Harper*Christian*
Resources

Not in It to Win It: Why Choosing Sides Sidelines the Church

Andy Stanley

Is it possible to disagree politically and love unconditionally? The reaction of evangelicals to political and cultural shifts in recent years revealed what they value most. Lurking beneath our Bible-laced rhetoric, faith claims, books, and sermons is a relentless drive to *WIN*!

But the church is not here to win. By every human measure, our Savior lost. On purpose. With a purpose. And we are his body. We are not in it to win anything. We are in it for something else entirely. That something else is what this book is about. You'll discover:

- How to take a stand the right way.
- How to view politics through the lens of faith.
- How the life of Jesus and his teaching applies to modern-day challenges in a fresh way.

Jesus never asked his followers to agree on everything. But he did call his followers to obey a new command: to love others in the same way he has loved us. Instead of asserting our rights or fighting for power, we need to begin asking ourselves: what does love require of me?

Available in stores and online!

Once upon a time there existed a version of our faith that the world found irresistible.

In this book and six-session study, Andy Stanley shows us how Jesus's arrival signaled that the Old Testament was fulfilled and its laws reduced to a single verb—love—to be applied to God, neighbor, and enemy. So, what is required if we want to follow Jesus's example and radically love the people around us? We almost always know the answer. The hard part is actually doing what love requires.

Book
9780310536970

Study Guide
9780310100492

DVD
9780310100515

Available now at your favorite bookstore, or streaming video on StudyGateway.com.

The New Rules for Love, Sex, and Dating

Andy Stanley

For anyone who is dating or thinking about marriage, pastor and bestselling author Andy Stanley shares practical, uncensored wisdom on avoiding mistakes in the present to help you avoid regrets in the future.

Single? Looking for the "right person"? Convinced that if you met the "right person" everything would turn out "right"? Think again.

In *The New Rules for Love, Sex, and Dating*, Andy Stanley explores the challenges, assumptions, and pitfalls associated with dating in the twenty-first century. This guide takes a fresh approach to dating and love in the modern era by turning the search for "the one" back onto the searcher, challenging you to ask yourself tough questions like:

- Am I the person that the person I'm looking for is looking for?
- Are the Bible's teachings about women relevant today?
- If sex is only physical, why is the pain of sexual sin so deep?

As you dig deep into Stanley's answers, you'll be equipped and empowered to step up and set a new standard for this generation by uncovering the things that create trouble in dating relationships and creating better habits now that will pay off later as you dive into married life.

Available in stores and online!

How to Be Rich

It's Not What You Have. It's What You Do With What You Have.

Andy Stanley

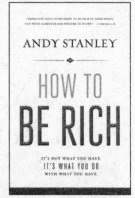

You probably don't feel rich. Rich is the other guy. Rich is having more than you currently have. But you can be rich and not feel it. And that's the problem. Andy Stanley is convinced that most of us are richer than we think. We just aren't very good at it. It's one thing to be rich. Andy wants us to be good at it!

> "How to Be Rich *lays out clear principles for carrying that load, making sure your wealth remains a blessing not just for you, but for your family and community for generations to come."*
>
> —DAVE RAMSEY, *New York Times* bestselling
> author and radio show host

Available in stores and online!